TA for Management

Making Life Work

THEODORE B. NOVEY

Transactional Analysis for Everybody Series

JALMAR Press, Inc.
391 Munroe Street
Sacramento, CA 95825

The help of the following sources is gratefully acknowledged:

W. Reddin for the Tri-Dimensional Leader-Effectiveness Model. Reproduced by special permission from the April, 1967 TRAINING AND DEVELOPMENT JOURNAL. Copyright 1967 by the American Society for Training and Development, Inc.

Franklin H. Ernst M.D. for the OK Corral sketch.

Dr. Robert R. Blake and Dr. Jane S. Mouton for the Managerial Grid figure from *The Managerial Grid,* by Robert R. Blake and Jane Srygley Mouton. Houston: Gulf Publishing Company, Copyright © 1964, page 10. Reproduced with permission.

Novey, Theodore B., "Middle-Escence and Management," *ITAA Journal,* 5:4, p. 366.

Library of Congress catalog card number: 76-19649
ISBN: 0-915190-05-2
Printed in the United States of America

Distributed to the retail book trade by Price/Stern/Sloan, Publishers

410 N. LaCienega, Los Angeles, CA 90048
(213) 657-6100

Educational, Religious distribution by JALMAR PRESS, INC.

391 Munroe St., Sacramento, CA 95825
(916) 481-1134

for JALMAR PRESS, INC.

Publisher — Alvyn M. Freed, Ph.D.

Editor-in-chief — John Dickinson Adams

Edited by Helen M. Friend
Cover art and book design by John T. Bookout

CONTENTS

Figures

Figures

Preface

Communication and interaction between individuals is the key substance of the life of an organization. The introduction of the theory of Transactional Analysis by Eric Berne and his co-workers in the last twenty years has provided a new and simpler framework with which to understand and facilitate change and growth in groups of any size from two to two million.

This manual arises from my experience in science and the management of scientific research for the past twenty-five years and from the cross-fertilization of this with training and experience in the field of Transactional Analysis. In moving from science to industrial management problems I learned that a basic question was: "How do you ask a question?" The answer to this question led to this book.

This book represents testimony to my transition from the world of basic science research in Physics to the world of human relationships. I have been immeasurably enriched by both of these fields and by the people who have helped me to make this transition. Some of the most significant of these are Morris and Natalie Haimowitz with whom I have learned and grown during the last six years; H. Dudley Wright, who took a chance on me and presented the question: "How do you ask a question?"; Alexey Shukin, who gave me all the flexibility that I needed for my re-education; Bruce Cork, who understood what I was about, and gave his support; Jerry Perlmutter, who offered me the challenge and warmth of his personality; Keith Hoover, who helped me find a place to grow and an ever abundant source of strokes; Elaine Novey, who has lived through these sometimes difficult years of transition with me and has given me her love and help including the editing of this book. I thank all of these and many others including scientific collaborators, students, patients and consultees from whom I have learned so much.

July, 1976
Downers Grove, Illinois

I.
People
to People
Communications

Theodore Novey is a management consultant to industrial organizations, hospitals and church groups. He has also been in private practice as a counselor for individuals and families, and has provided advanced training in Transactional Anaysis for professionals.

Dr. Novey was a Senior Physicist engaged in basic research in Nuclear Physics for Argonne National Laboratory for twenty-five years.

He earned his Ph.D. in physical chemistry at the University of Chicago and his M. S. in Counseling Psychology from George Williams College. He is a clinical member and a provisional teaching member of the International Transactional Analysis Association, a fellow of the American Physical Society and an Associate Member of the American Psychological Association. Dr. Novey makes his home in Downers Grove, Illinois.

Chapter One:
THE PROBLEM OF COMMUNICATION

Communication and the Analysis of Transactions

The sensory capabilities of human beings are wonderfully sensitive and wide ranging. Our ability to sense the world around us, to store the information we get and transmit it to others, has allowed the development of the highly sophisticated civilization that we experience today.

The process of communication between humans involves all of the senses that are presently known—hearing, sight, touch, smell, and taste—and may involve other extra-sensory perceptions not yet established.

Any theory of human communication must allow for the simultaneous use of these senses in controlling human response. In order for a personality theory of behavior to be useful it must allow a means for relatively simple classification of the enormous amount of data transmitted in human contact and it must be able to predict results of human communication and human interaction.

Human communication can be defined and analyzed via the concept of the transaction, that is: I "say" something to you—verbally or non-verbally; you "say" something to me—verbally or non-verbally. Human feeling, thinking, and behavior express themselves in the transactions between people or, as we shall see later, in the internal transactions between ego states within a person.

The value of any theory depends on the simplicity of its assumptions and the number of characteristic properties which one needs to know about in order to classify the data and to predict the results of future interactions.

One simple and elegant theory for explaining human behavior was proposed by Eric Berne in 1953 when he developed his personality theory called "Structural and Transactional Analysis."[1] Berne's theory analyzes human behavior by analyzing the transactions between people and within the individual's mental process. Behavior change then reflects itself in a change in the kind, quality, or quantity of transactions which will occur. Conversely, the way to change my behavior is to change the way I transact.

Berne's theory, based on the wealth of developmental psychology and the Freudian tradition of analytic psychology, was aimed at extracting a simple set of concepts which would form a simple theoretical model. This model would serve as a structure for classifying the enormous variety of human behavior. One important goal of Berne's was to eliminate complicated language and to limit the theoretical language to a few words which can be most easily understood at the human feeling level. Then the separation of humans into expert and non-expert groups in terms of their ability to understand and change human behavior can be minimized. This break with the tradition in the field of psychology and psychotherapy has at the same time cleared away much of the mystery and fear of human feelings and irritated psychologists and psychiatrists brought up in the traditional language of behavior and personality.

The mark of progress in scientific theory has always been associated with the introduction of simplifying assumptions and aesthetic elegance of the theoretical structure. There is something very satisfying in simplicity. Good medicine doesn't have to taste bad.

In this chapter a summary of the Transactional Analysis (TA) theory and the PARENT-ADULT-CHILD (PAC) personality model will be presented. This theory is aimed at explaining human behavior and examining the communications or transactions that occur between people.

States of the Ego

In the past thirty years the concept and phenomenology of ego states in human experience have been developed by many researchers and clinicians. An ego state appears as a coherent set or system of feelings relating to a given life situation and a set of related behavior patterns. Alternatively, an ego state can be described as a set of internal feelings or thoughts that result in a characteristic set of behavior patterns.

The phenomena of ego states have been investigated experimentally by Penfield[2] through experiments in which stimulation of the brain revived whole sets of memories complete with the re-experiencing of the feelings associated with the memories. Penfield did not call these re-experienced behavior patterns ego states, but they are closely connected to ego states as discussed in TA theory.

Federn's ego psychology was the first theory to stress, on psychiatric grounds, that psychological reality was based on complete and discrete ego states.[3]

Weiss, who followed Federn, extended and detailed the evidence for the existence of ego states. He describes the ego state as ". . . the actually experienced reality of one's mental and bodily ego with the contents of the lived-through period. . . ."[4]

Like other natural phenomena which begin to be recognized by a science, the concepts of the ego states were seen in part and in many views by a number of scientists and clinicians. Eric Berne built his theory of human behavior from the concepts he learned from Penfield, Federn, Weiss, and others. He has detailed this historical development in his first book, **Transactional Analysis in Psychotherapy.**

PARENT, ADULT, CHILD EGO STATES

As Berne says, "Everyone was a child once." The set of feelings and behavior of that time forms the basis for the CHILD ego state. Each person has had parents or some powerful humans in their lives in their early years of development, otherwise he or she could not have lived through the years of complete or partial dependency. The behavior patterns and feelings of these people form the basis for the PARENT ego state.

Everyone has a mental structure which allows him to take in the results of his or her contacts with the real world, to evaluate this data, to compare this data with data fed into the brain from his or her parents, and to make decisions as to what to do in the here and now. The capacity and speed of action of this structure may have genetic limitations, but everyone has the capacity to control his or her actions using this ADULT ego state.

Description of the ego states will include not only the feelings and feeling levels experienced but also the behavior emitted by the person: facial expression, words used, tonal quality, body position and movement, and sensitivity to aural and other sensory stimulation.

The basic assumption of the PAC model is that a person is at any time primarily in one of three ego states called PARENT, ADULT, or CHILD which comprise the personality characteristics shown in Figure 1. Transactions between people can thus be understood as communication from an ego state of person A to an ego state of person B and are designated as ADULT-ADULT or A-A, PARENT-CHILD or P-C, CHILD-CHILD or C-C, etc. Further details about this classification and the rules of communication are given in Chapter Two.

EGO STATE SHIFTS

In the mature, well-functioning person these behavior patterns are readily identified, and there is a minimum of confusion between ego states. The person can shift quickly from one ego state to another and is aware of which state he is in. An observer can identify the ego state from the tone of voice, facial appearance, words used, and body position and posture. For example, in a typical Critical PARENT state, the person's expression is grim and set and often the forefinger is extended for emphasis on the "You." A Nurturing PARENT can be characterized by a warm, helping attitude, "good" advice giving, caring and nurturing,

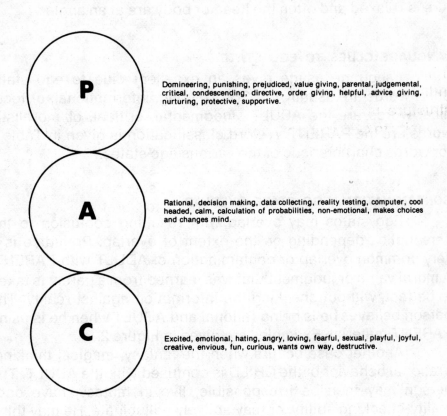

Domineering, punishing, prejudiced, value giving, parental, judgemental, critical, condescending, directive, order giving, helpful, advice giving, nurturing, protective, supportive.

Rational, decision making, data collecting, reality testing, computer, cool headed, calm, calculation of probabilities, non-emotional, makes choices and changes mind.

Excited, emotional, hating, angry, loving, fearful, sexual, playful, joyful, creative, envious, fun, curious, wants own way, destructive.

Fig. 1. Qualities of the PARENT, ADULT and CHILD

mothering or "smothering" attitude. In the ADULT state the person looks calm, cool, unemotional. His or her voice is even and colorless. Hands and body are relatively at rest. In the CHILD state the voice is animated. There is more body movement. Posture is relaxed and often the head or body are at an angle.

LANGUAGE CLUES TO EGO STATE

Language usage gives an excellent clue to ego state. Short words are usually the CHILD. Long, informational, or technical words are the ADULT. Judgmental, critical, or moralistic words are the PARENT. A word classification is given in Table 1 for words characteristic of the various ego states.

CONTAMINATION: EGO STATE OVERLAP

Ego states may overlap with resulting confusion to the personality, depending on the extent of overlap. Prejudice is a very common overlap or contamination of ADULT with PARENT. A moral value or judgment that was learned from a parent is taken to be fact, without checking the information against reality. The person believes he is being rational and ADULT when he is using PARENT material. Examples are given in Figure 2.

Another case occurs when the fantasy, magical thinking, irrational behavior of the CHILD is confused with the ADULT. The person may then be irresponsible, live in fantasy, have poor reality-checking ability, or may actively hallucinate. He may think he really hears or sees something and acts in a "rational" way based on irrational data. (See Figure 3.)

These contaminations of ego states become more severe as the personality is distorted by neurosis or psychosis. In the latter state the ADULT or PARENT ego states may not be used by the person at all.

STRUCTURE OF THE CHILD

The most powerful and controlling part of the personality is the CHILD ego state. In the long run, it is the emotions and feelings that the person responds to. The CHILD is the only ego state present at birth. The CHILD develops rapidly in the first five

P A C WORD CLASSIFICATIONS

PARENT   Right, wrong, bad, good, immoral, moral, duty, should, ought, upright, childish, peculiar, can't, don't, shouldn't, insist, demand, critical, punish, care, support, teach, protect, help, order, values, righteous, judgment, ridiculous, silly, artistic, thief, careless, interfering, obsession, furious, approve, disapprove, thorough, lust, agreeable, pleasant, vice, sin, inheritance, culture, cultured

ADULT   Data, reasonable, calculate, estimate, decide, transform, wide, narrow, thin, stretch, computer, facts, reality, test, adjust, inquisitive, travel, interest, substance, anger, move, homogenize, obtain, occupation, danger, result, gestate, automobile, one, two, three, add, divide, alimentation, masticate, odor, intuit, perspire, self, myself, property, search, pain, accept

CHILD   Want, will, let's, won't, grab, fun, run, hop, skip, nosey, carefree, steal, dare, now, sad, mad, glad, sex, skin, body, curious, laugh, jump, hate, shake, take, car, food, eat, smell, guess, sweat, me, mine, funny, ouch, oh, see, O. K., talk, taste, here, give, bite, lick

Table I. PARENT, ADULT, and CHILD Words

9

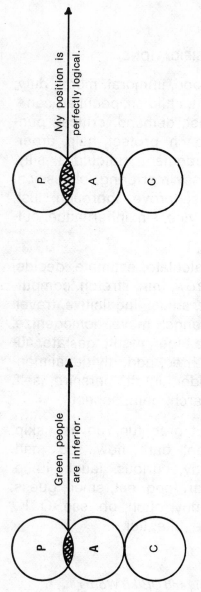

Figure 2. PARENT-ADULT contamination

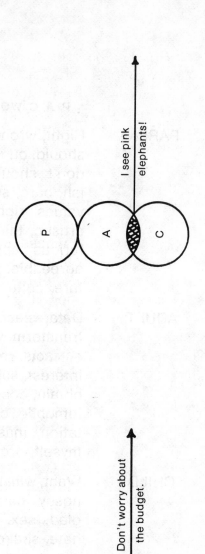

Figure 3. ADULT-CHILD contamination

years of life and becomes the repository of its parents' verbal and non-verbal communications, which are so powerful in determining the life style of the developing person. The CHILD ego state is also the source of the most intuitive and creative thinking, and as such is a crucial part of the personality.

In order to discuss the structure of the CHILD it is convenient to divide this ego state into three parts: the Adapted CHILD, the Little Professor, and the Natural CHILD. (See Figure 4.)

The Adapted CHILD is most closely allied with the concept of the Superego from classical analytic theory. The direct, cultural, moral, fearful, angry, and similar feelings about the world that parents carry in their own Adapted CHILD are focused in this part of the CHILD. These messages are the first to be transmitted to the child, verbally or non-verbally, when in the early years of life the most powerful point of contact is between the CHILD of the parents and the CHILD of the child.

The Little Professor is the part of the CHILD that develops to solve the problems of getting its needs filled. This part, as indicated by its name, is very intuitive and creative in solving these problems and becomes evident very quickly in young children. The Little Professor is not the same as the ADULT ego state because it operates many times without good rational reality contact, and relies on fantasy, intuition, or magical thinking in coming to decisions.

The Natural CHILD is the natural part of the child, with all of the genetic influences on feelings, activity levels, moods, responsiveness, and so on. This remains the source of basic feelings and wants that have no morality, but only a desire for fulfillment and a violent reaction to frustration.

These three parts of the CHILD are diagrammed in Figure 4. (This is called second order PAC, or second order structural analysis of this ego state.)

Strokes

How does the structure of the personality known as PAC come about?

In the first few years of life, primarily from birth to five

11

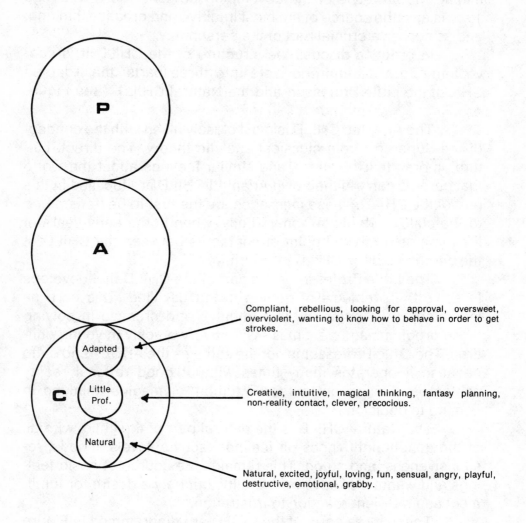

Figure 4. Structure of the CHILD ego state

P

A

C

Adapted — Compliant, rebellious, looking for approval, oversweet, overviolent, wanting to know how to behave in order to get strokes.

Little Prof. — Creative, intuitive, magical thinking, fantasy planning, non-reality contact, clever, precocious.

Natural — Natural, excited, joyful, loving, fun, sensual, angry, playful, destructive, emotional, grabby.

years of age, the infant and child gets the first and most important lessons on how to stay alive, and how to get strokes (physical strokes or comfortable feelings or uncomfortable feelings) from the life-supporting people around it—usually the parents. These lessons come verbally or non-verbally in response to the child's activities, resulting in positive or negative reinforcement which guide the child's learning and development. In the process, because of the close and powerful dependency, deep beliefs of the parents are transmitted to the child—essentially tape recorded into the child's brain; the child must and wants to please its parents and will distort its own needs if necessary in order to do this.

The youngster must get stroked by its mother and father in order to live; therefore, it accepts their Adapted CHILD messages and adapts its own personality and reactions to this via the clever, intuitive, creative, precocious child—the Little Professor—who is very sensitive to its parents' feelings and learns what to do to make Daddy smile or Mommy pay attention and not leave.

Figure 5 shows how the deep-lying behavior patterns of the parents, which reside inside the Adapted CHILD of the parent, are transmitted and accepted by the child.

This Little Professor remains the intuitive, clever, synthesizing part of the personality, and if not decommissioned by too much internal pressure to adapt, becomes the core of the creative personality. The connection between creativity and spontaneous child-like actions of many people is easy to see. Creativity is associated with the CHILD ego state—in particular with the Little Professor.

Reinforcement, positive and negative, is widely recognized as a basic force in human development. In TA **stroke** is the word used to describe the unit of recognition given by a person to himself or by one person to another. Recognition is essential to life.

Case Illustration

A growing organization had chronic space problems. One department head asked to use the space, he was rebuffed and there was much talk about giving and getting strokes; during some group exercises the two department heads had a chance to talk directly to each other and establish some CHILD-CHILD communication. A week later the first supervisor came in to the second's office and said"I have a stroke for you," and handed him the key to the room he needed.

13

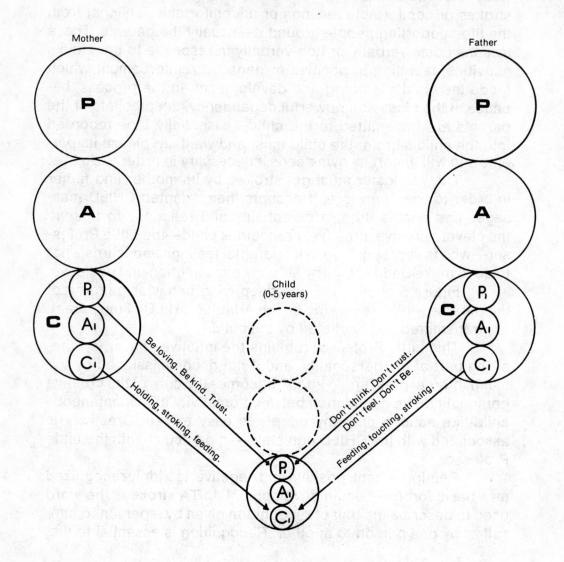

Mother

P

A

C
P_1
A_1
C_1

Be loving. Be kind. Trust.

Holding, stroking, feeding.

Child
(0-5 years)

P_1
A_1
C_1

Father

P

A

C
P_1
A_1
C_1

Don't think. Don't trust.
Don't feel. Don't Be.

Feeding, touching, stroking.

Fig. 5.   The little professor (A 1) knows how to maximize stroking by
accepting rules of behavior from the parents.

14

The youngster prefers to work for positive strokes. If it cannot get these because the parents are tired, hungry, angry, unhappy, or don't know how to give positive strokes—never having learned how from their parents—then the child will settle for negative strokes, criticism, scolding, hitting, and so on. Negative strokes are not as good as positive, but they are better than nothing. To be ignored is to die, figuratively or literally.

The two basic kinds of stroking are self-stroking and stroking from others. This corresponds to feelings of self-esteem and esteem by others. Both are essential for effective human functioning. A person with low self-esteem, in other words, low self-stroking, may seek to compensate for this by getting much external recognition; this recognition, however, is not very satisfying. The achievement of fame and the applause of thousands or millions does not counteract the inner pain of those who can only criticize and never be satisfied with themselves.

Conversely, no amount of self-esteem and self-stroking will enable a person to escape the loneliness which results from being cut off from recognition and stroking by others.

Negative stroking from oneself or others will keep a person alive, but negative strokes are not a satisfactory substitute for positive strokes. Negative strokes simply don't feel good to the human system and good is the way the Natural CHILD wants to feel.

A third kind of stroking involves conditional strokes. These involve acceptance **if**— and imply that a person is only of value if he or she does something for somebody else. Conditional strokes confuse acceptance and OKness as a human being with liking or approving what is done.

Straight statements would be:

    a) You are OK and I don't like what you are doing.

    b) I respect your right to be your own person, but I don't think we can work together productively.

    c) You have your needs from this job and I have mine, and I don't think that you are meeting my needs or this company's needs.

Conditional strokes would be:
   a) Be a good guy and work harder.
   b) If you'd produce more, we could be friends.
   c) If only you weren't so lazy (I'd like you).

Some positive, negative, and conditional strokes are diagrammed in Figure 6.

As the Little Professor learns how to get strokes from the parents, and what kinds it can get, a pattern of behavior is set up. In later life the mature person will work for positive or negative strokes of one kind or another, depending on its early education. For example, one employee will work for, expect, and enjoy positive recognition, while another will arrange things and relationships so that he will get criticism and other negative strokes and will get a seemingly perverse satisfaction out of complaining. This is not perverse. He was taught that negative strokes were what he could get; as a result, he does not know how to accept positive strokes and hence rejects them—leading to more negative strokes.

Most people work for a mixture of positive and negative strokes. Contentment, happiness, a sense of fulfillment, feelings of love, self-actualization, and completeness are some of the words that describe the feelings of persons who are giving many positive strokes to themselves and to others, and are getting many positive strokes from others.

Time Structure

The ways people go about getting strokes lead to a classification of the ways that people use their life-time. All human behavior can be classified into six groups:

   1. Withdrawal
   2. Rituals
   3. Pastimes
   4. Activity or Work
   5. Games (in the TA sense)
   6. Intimacy

16

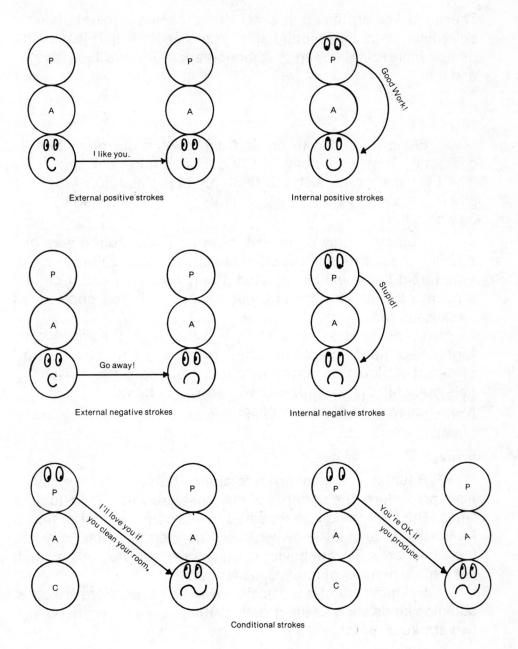

External positive strokes

Internal positive strokes

External negative strokes

Internal negative strokes

Conditional strokes

Figure 6. Three kinds of strokes

These classes are listed in order of increasing stroke-obtaining potentiality and, correspondingly, in the order which leaves the person increasingly open to rejection and hurt, and thus danger and fear.

WITHDRAWAL

Being by and with oneself and away from other human contact is an essential part of living. I need a certain amount of time by myself to be alone to think my thoughts undisturbed by others. I decide to withdraw for a time and am free to do so or to be with others.

Perhaps I stay by myself, drawing away from others and refusing the approaches of others because I lack self-esteem, or I am afraid that I will be rejected. I am "shy." I spend a certain amount of time withdrawing, not because of free choice, but because of fear.

In the most extreme case of withdrawal, the world is so frightening that I do not know how to get **any** safe strokes, so I close off all lines of communication. Nothing gets in. Nothing gets out. This extreme form of withdrawal is found in the people in the back wards of mental hospitals.

RITUAL

Ritual is the name given to human behavior that follows a fixed procedure; the patterns of response are well known to both sides. The pattern can be repeated exactly any number of times. All parties to a ritual know what will happen and how they will feel afterwards. This behavior is quite safe and provides a small but certain number of strokes, usually positive.

Religious ritual is the best known; however, there are other common kinds such as the greeting ritual between two people. A two-stroke ritual is:
Hello.
Hello.
How are you?
Fine, thanks.
In these two transactions each person gets and gives two strokes.

This can be easily extended to many-stroke rituals. The essential point is that once a ritual is established between two people, each side expects the same number of strokes at each daily meeting. Any change in the ritual length is noted with uneasiness. If the ritual is interrupted for a few days then at the first meeting the people will expect the strokes to be made up by a longer ritual after which they can be content to go back to the original ritual.

There are many other rituals in social life. In organizational life there are also many—such as, the way meetings get underway or even how they proceed, in other words, the agenda. A certain amount of ritual adds to the comfort of living. Indeed, many people find a great comfort from religious ritual. If decision-making is done by ritual or if ritual takes so much time that there is little time or place for other kinds of transactions, then the organization will become stereotyped, rigid, and ineffective.

In scientific and social life as well as in business life, there is a well-known ritualized procedure for beginning a conversation. Each side asks the other in turn the questions: What's new? How is your family? Where are you working or living now? What kind of research, work, gardening, and so on have you been doing? After this ritualized conversation, the parties can separate feeling somewhat satisfied—or, they may decide to go to a somewhat riskier level of communication: Pastimes, Games, or intimacy.

PASTIMES

The next level of behavior, called Pastiming, involves people in transactions on a superficial level. One talks and exchanges recognition strokes, but on a relatively safe level.

A typical Pastime is "Ain't It Awful." This is a PARENT type of Pastime in which the two parties exchange statements on the poor state of something—kids, cars, politics, business profits, and the like. The discussion concerns how it isn't like it used to be, how this needs changing, how that is getting in a bad state, how cars don't last like they used to.

Some common Pastimes are: languages, cars (What kind of a car do you have?), houses, maids (It's so difficult to get good

19

help these days!). In the work situation some additional Pastimes are: What's new? Ever been to . . .? Who won (sports)? How was the flight? Robert's Rules of Order, the welcoming speech, and martinis (I like mine 5 to 1).

Pastiming often occurs at the beginning of a conversation or a conference while waiting for the real events to begin. It is also used in probing another person gently to see if it is safe to go on to Games or intimacy.

ACTIVITY OR WORK

Human beings spend most of their lifetime in this way. **Work** for money is the standard way by which people obtain food, housing, and other necessities. In addition, work is a source of both internal and external strokes because a person feels useful and approved of by his own PARENT and by the societal PARENT when he produces something for the society. Work also has its play and fun components which the CHILD enjoys. This component is more clearly seen in the other part of this class called **activity** which includes sports, hobbies, golf, sailing, football, fishing, travel, and joining and participating in various community organizations or activities.

This class brings many strokes, positive and negative. It also is less safe in that the person puts himself up to be compared to others and perhaps is rejected. We compete for the strokes which are limited in the economy. Some get many more strokes than others because of natural ability, training, or education. Others get only negative strokes because of accident of birth, patterns set by early training, and so on.

GAMES

At this level of behavior, important strokes, mostly negative, are sought and exchanged. It is here that the early behavior patterns established in primary family relationships are re-utilized to get the kind of strokes that the person learned he was entitled to and was able to get when he was very young.

The person has established his Script—life style **or life** plan—and sets about carrying it out in straight ways, if **possible—**

20

but in any way—devious or dishonest, to himself or others—in order to get the things that he feels he needs in order to live.

The patterns of transactions which a person uses, utilizing devious methods of manipulating the other persons in his life, are called Games. They are characterized by the presence of a repetitive pattern of transactions, involving secret transactions, and conclude by each person receiving strokes from the other, usually negative.

Games have been well classified and described by Berne in his book, **Games People Play.** The results of Games are not lighthearted, as they may conclude in suicide or murder in the extreme cases.

The basic Game that can often be seen in childhood in varying intensities is "Mine is Bigger (or Better) than Yours." This Game reflects the early messages given to children carrying the feeling "You are Not-OK," "Don't feel good about yourself." The goal of the Game is to engage in a competition where the child has a large chance of losing. He then gets the original message of not being the best or OK confirmed, gets some negative strokes (bad feelings) which confirm the mother's or father's message and produce the perverse pleasure of agreeing with the parent at his own disadvantage. He gets stroked by the PARENT in his head for being what the real-life parent wanted.

Some Games often seen in work situations and in organizations are:

WHY DON'T YOU — YES, BUT
(WDYYB)

This is based on the early message $P_1 \rightarrow P_1$ (the parent's P_1 to to the child's P_1): "Don't take care of yourself." In order to obtain approval from his mother and father this youngster learned to not decide for himself but to ask them what to do. He was not able to take care of himself and grow into a mature individual; and thus, he is likely angry about this. The anger appears in the pleasure of frustrating his mother and father or the PARENT in others by asking for advice and then having a reason why he can't follow the advice.

As indicated by the name, this Game starts when advice is asked by the CHILD. If the PARENT is hooked into the Game, the other person says, "Why don't you . . . ," followed by some good advice. A sure indication that the Game has begun is given by the reply, "Yes, but I can't do that because . . . ," and some good reason or other is given. This Game ends when the PARENT gets frustrated and angry. He says "I was only trying to help," and takes away bad feelings as does the Game initiator who gets his bad feelings by being criticized, kicked, or fired.

The way to counter the Game WDYYB is to avoid the PARENT reply, "Why don't you." If, however, this reply is given, then as soon as the "yes, but" is detected, switch into the ADULT state and say, for example, "What do you want to do?" ADULT-CHILD state might ask, "What are the possibilities?" Or use the ADULT-ADULT state and refuse to get hooked into the PARENT. The use of positive strokes in order to encourage the other to use his ADULT may lead to a change in behavior, for example "You've got a good head. What are *your* ideas on how to solve this problem?"

As Games require two to play, the person getting hooked into this Game is most likely the one who feels the most comfortable in the PARENT state and has an inclination to play "I'm only trying to help."

COURTROOM

"Courtroom" is a sibling rivalry Game and starts in a family in which there are not enough strokes to go around. The children need more strokes and will use devious ways to get them, usually negative; parents can usually be annoyed into giving scoldings, punishments, and so on.

In an organization two people will come to the boss with complaints about each other. "He said . . ." one will say and will go into a long story about what each person said. The other person involved will do the same. The boss is ostensibly supposed to be the fair judge. If the boss is hooked into being the judge (PARENT), he will dispense positive strokes to one and negative strokes to the other—or perhaps he will give negative strokes to each of them. The judge gets his bad feelings when the whole process repeats itself and he realizes that he has not solved anything. Two responses from the boss may end this Game, at least with him as a participant.

1. ADULT-ADULT: How can we solve this problem?
2. ADULT-CHILD: How can you get more of the recognition (strokes) that you deserve?

Some other Games, the idea of which can be obtained from the name and the underlying $P_i \rightarrow P_i$ injunctions, are revealed in script messages from parents.

SCRIPT MESSAGE	GAME
You can't trust anyone!	NIGYSOB: Now I've got you, you SOB
Don't be satisfied with yourself!	Harried
Be helpless!	Look how hard I'm trying
Don't expect gratitude (strokes!)	I'm only trying to help you
Don't think!	Stupid

INTIMACY OR OPENNESS

Intimacy or openness is on the opposite end of the scale from withdrawal and offers the most possibilities for obtaining positive strokes. Intimacy also carries the most danger and the most sensitivity to being rejected and hurt. Covering a much wider range of possible situations than the usual sexual meaning of the word, intimacy implies CHILD-CHILD communication and interaction. Intimacy is achieved in the transactions between people who are sufficiently autonomous to use all three ego states as they choose. They are:

PARENT: Non-judgmental, non-critical, nurturing, supportive

ADULT: Autonomous, flexible, rational, in contact with reality, decision-making, data-collecting

CHILD: Aware of feelings and needs, pleasure loving, with self-esteem

In relationships between open human beings, decisions are made by their ADULTs with due consideration of the facts, the input of culture and traditions from the PARENTs, and the needs and wants of the CHILD.

A relationship has the possibilities of nine transactions between ego states—diagrammed in Figure 7, p. 34. The more of these transactions which are present, the more complete the intimacy which is possible and comfortable.

23

Life Positions and Life Styles

The way one's time is structured, in terms of the classifications in the last section, represents decisions made by the individual as to the best way to get the strokes needed for survival. In this section some of the types of decisions that children make at about age five or six will be discussed. Later on in their lives these decisions will affect their response to the external world. Based upon the kinds and numbers of strokes that children receive in their families, they develop attitudes about themselves and about the rest of the world. These can be categorized quite concisely in the phrases[5]:

I'm OK.　　　or　　I'm Not-OK.
You're OK.　　or　　You're Not-OK.

This set of choices leads to one of four basic positions.

► *I'M OK AND YOU'RE OK:* This is the result of adequate positive stroking and says that the child feels OK about himself or herself, and is entitled and able to get what he wants and needs in life.

► *I'M NOT-OK BUT YOU'RE OK:* This is the result of a lack of positive stroking or deprivation and the substitution of negative stroking or criticism. The child sees that others can get positive strokes and love, but somehow he doesn't, so that means something must be wrong with him and not with other people. He or she decides that he is Not-OK and will have to settle for a life within this basic assumption. Then he will seek negative strokes as a consolation prize and will take a basic loser outlook on life.

► *I'M OK AND YOU'RE NOT-OK:* This is usually the position taken by children who have been heavily criticized or punished or been abused physically by beating, torture, sexual abuse, or exploitation. They decide that they can't be bad enough to deserve such terrible treatment and so they must be blameless and it is the others who are Not-OK. Children who are beaten often grow up to be parents who beat their children, criminals, or psychopaths who abuse others.

► *I'M NOT-OK AND YOU'RE NOT-OK:* This is the extreme position taken by children who get few strokes, positive **or** negative. They are taught that their needs are not important, that parents' needs come first, and that the world is a scary place. They decide that they will neither give nor receive strokes, and withdraw into a world of their own— a schizophrenic world in the extreme cases.

There are all variations of intensity in these positions and most people experience one or another of these positions at some time; however, when one position is dominant, then a life style is apparent.

The I'm OK, You're OK position is the position of the winner who is getting on with life.

The I'm Not-OK but You're OK position is a loser position and is characterized by depression and hopelessness.

The I'm OK and You're Not-OK position blames everything on the others and in the extreme case is a paranoid position.

The I'm Not-OK and You're Not-OK position is a withdrawn position and in the extreme case is a schizophrenic position.

Script, Counterscript and Life Style

When the boy or girl has collected some ideas about life as seen from his family experience for a few years, he may at the age of four to six begin to develop fixed ideas about what his life will be like. If living has been loving and relatively free from pain and he has had adequate positive stroking, he will not make many long-range decisions but will live flexibly with many choices of life style and changes in life style.

If he or she has experienced a lack of positive strokes and has had to adapt to many destructive **Don'ts,** such as Don't be, Don't think for yourself, Don't feel, Don't talk, Don't ask for yourself, and so on, then he will make a decision about his life position. He will begin to write a story in his mind about what his life will have to be like.

This story or Script will at first be a simple story line. Perhaps like Oedipus, "I'm going to kill my father and marry my mother"; or less dramatically, "I'm not going to think and make decisions and take care of myself and I'll be dead when I'm thirty"; or "I'll manage to get along on almost no strokes and nothing much will happen in my life." As the person grows, this Script will be elaborated to include the types of characters he will fill his life with, in order to carry out the Script line.

If a woman has decided that she won't get many strokes, she may develop a Mother Hubbard Script and have many children so that all of the strokes will go to them and to her husband and there will not be any left for her. There have been a number of books written on scripts including **Games Alcoholics Play: The Analysis of Life Scripts** and **Scripts People Live** by Claude Steiner and **What Do You Say After You Say Hello,** by Eric Berne. "Women's Scripts" have been described by Hoagy Wyckoff.[6]

The rigidity of the life Script depends upon the number and intensity of the injunctions or **Don'ts** experienced by the youngster. As he grows older, he hears other messages from parents and culture, usually urging him on to success, fame, hard work, sacrifice, or other culturally accepted norms. If he has been deciding on a life Script that is painful, then he may attempt to build an alternate way of life based upon these later messages, and will write a Counterscript or alternate life style which seems to counteract the Script. These successful, achievement-types of story lines are called Counterscripts. The person may live for a long time or even all his or her life in Counterscript with only occasional reminders from internal feelings, that underneath the success lies some pain and unresolved problems.

Counterscript may give way in times of tension, crisis, or temporary failure, and the person will suddenly revert to his original script.

The onset of depressions or suicide, or drug or alcohol abuse during these times, is an indication of a transfer from Counterscript to Script. As the CHILD is the power behind the personality, the Script messages are the most important; and when a person wants to change, he must first change or rewrite his basic Script before attempting to change the Counterscript. There is danger, for example, in encounter or therapy groups where people work at an emotional level without adequately trained leaders. If a person's defenses or Counterscript are penetrated by the group pressure and emotional intensity, he may flip to a destructive Script position; without adequate therapist protection he may decide on self-destruction or going crazy, if this was called for by his original Script.

The change of Scripts or life style is the primary goal of Transactional Analysis. The analysis in a group setting concentrates on finding out what the original injunctions and decisions were. Then, with adequate protection by the therapist's PARENT, the person makes piecemeal contracts to change his Script, to negate the original injunctions, to begin leading a different life—and to get reinforcing strokes for the change from those around him.

Change is difficult because it means doing something different from what one's parents said to do at an early age, so there is much fear and anger associated with change. Once the change process has successfully begun and the person knows that he can face his internal feelings and not feel guilty or bad, then he will be willing to make further changes that lead toward getting more positive strokes for himself or herself.

Conclusion

The usefulness of the PAC model of human behavior lies in its ability to help sort out the large mass of data coming and going between people. If we can get an idea of what is going on, we can know how to direct our efforts in the directions we want to go, in order to maximize, for example, human values, human relationships, and desirable productivity.

The basic data needed are:
1. What ego states are in control?
2. What kind of stroking is going on?
3. What is the time structure?
4. What Games are going on?

b) What fantasies do you carry around in your head about the big deal coming? About vacation and work? About your relationship with others? About the world?

Which part of the fantasy is wishful thinking and which part is connected with reality?

5. What are the life positions of the people involved?

6. What are the Scripts and Counterscripts of the people involved?

7. What changes are desired by the people involved?

We then know a great deal about the variables of the problem, and we have some good ideas on how to intervene and on what must be changed in order to reach the goals agreed upon.

Applications and Exercises

1. EGO STATES

a) During the week while talking to workers or employees, check on which ego-state you are using.

b) Select two or three of the people around you and identify their ego-states from their words, tone of voice, facial expression, and body movement. Watch for ego-state switches.

c) When you are about to make a decision, stop for a minute and ask yourself: What is my CHILD feeling? What is my ADULT thinking or concluding? What is my PARENT opinion?

2. CONTAMINATION

a) List any strong opinions that you may have about members of the opposite sex, other races or religions, workers in other fields, politicians, movie stars, and so on. Think about the facts behind each opinion. Do you have real information? Are you reflecting someone else's opinion?

3. YOUR CHILD

Locate yourself on the following scales for these questions:

a) How concerned are you about adapting to the desires of others?

b) To the extent that you react to the demands of others, do you feel compliant or rebellious?

c) How much chance do you get to use your creative, intuitive self?

d) How free do you feel to be openly playful, angry, sexy, joyful, sad?

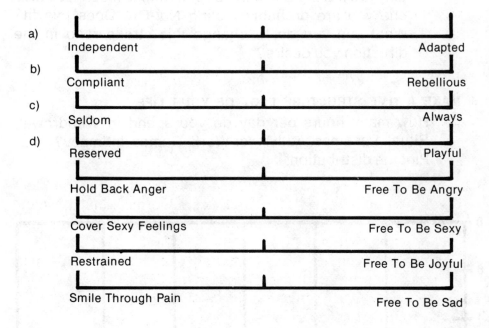

a) Independent	Adapted
b) Compliant	Rebellious
c) Seldom	Always
d) Reserved	Playful
Hold Back Anger	Free To Be Angry
Cover Sexy Feelings	Free To Be Sexy
Restrained	Free To Be Joyful
Smile Through Pain	Free To Be Sad

4. STROKE RATIO

a) List the important people or groups of people in your life.

b) Estimate the number of minutes per day that you get

positive strokes from each person or group of persons. Add up the total minutes.

c) Estimate the number of minutes per day that you get negative strokes from each person or group of persons. Add up the total minutes.

d) Estimate the number of minutes per day that you get conditional strokes from each person or group of persons. Add up the total minutes and divide by two.

e) Calculate your stroke ratio:

$$\text{Stroke ratio} = \frac{\text{total positive stroke minutes}}{\text{total negative stroke minutes} + \frac{1}{2} \text{ total conditional stroke minutes}}$$

f) If the stroke ratio is much greater than one, you probably are feeling OK. If the stroke ratio is much less than one you are probably feeling Not-OK. Does this fit? What can you do to change this stroke ratio in the direction you desire?

5. MAKE A TIME STRUCTURE PLOT OF YOUR LIFE

How many hours per day do you spend in Withdrawal, Ritual, Pastimes, Activity or Work, Games, Intimacy? Plot the distribution.

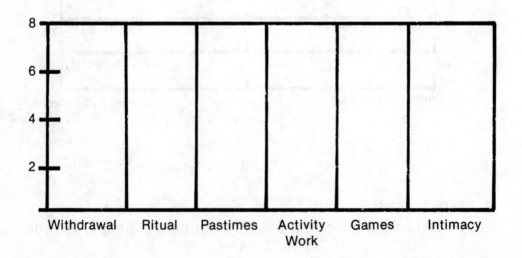

Do you want to make any changes in the way you spend your time? What are the changes? How will you go about making the changes? When will you start?

6. GAMES

What repetitive life situations do you find yourself getting into that end up in negative strokes for all concerned? At what point do you get hooked into angry or other unpleasant feelings? How can you change the situation so as to get positive strokes or at least avoid the negative?

7. MAKE A LIFE POSITION PLOT

How many hours a day do you spend in each position?

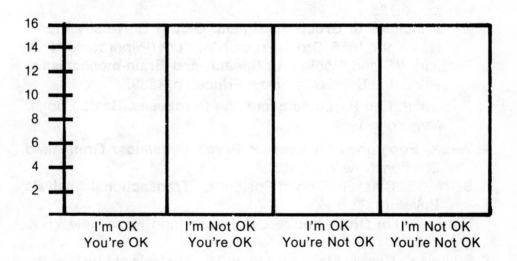

Examine your principal position. When did you decide that position was yours? How would you go about changing this decision if you want to?

8. LIFE SCRIPT

    a) What are the Dont's and Do's by which you run your life? Who said these to you?

b) How do you feel that your life is supposed to go?

c) What do you say to yourself in times of joy, anger, crisis?

d) What do you want to change about your life style? What resources, people, time, planning is required to bring about these changes?

REFERENCES

1. Berne, E. **Transactional Analysis in Psychotherapy.** Grove Press, New York, 1961.
   The Structure and Dynamics of Organization and Groups. J. B. Lippincott Company, Philadelphia, 1963. Grove Press (Paperback), New York, 1966.
   Games People Play. Grove Press, New York, 1964 (Paperback) 1967.
   Principles of Group Treatment. Oxford University Press, New York, 1966. Grove Press, New York (Paperback) 1968.

2. Penfield, W. and Robias, L. **Speech and Brain-mechanisms.** Princeton University Press, Princeton, 1959.

3. Federn, P. **Ego Psychology and the Psychoses.** Basic Books, New York, 1952.

4. Weiss, Edoardo. **Principles of Psychodynamics.** Grune and Stratton, New York, 1950.

5. Berne, E. "Classification of Positions." **Transactional Analysis Bulletin** 1:23, 1962.
   Harris, T. **I'm OK — You're OK.** Harper and Row, New York, 1967.

6. Steiner, C. **Games Alcoholics Play: The Analysis of Life Scripts.** Grove Press, New York, 1971.
   Steiner, C. **Scripts People Live.** Grove Press, New York, 1974.
   Berne, E. **What Do You Say After You Say Hello?** Grove Press, New York, 1971.
   Wyckoff, H. "The Stroke Economy in Women's Scripts." **Transactional Analysis Journal** 1:3, July, 1971.

Chapter Two:
GATHERING INFORMATION

How to Ask a Question

The way a question is asked in great part determines how it will be answered. Not only are the words used important, but the tone quality, the facial expression at the time, the body position and hand movements, the eyes, skin color, and many other hardly noticeable non-verbal communications—experienced all at the same time by the person receiving the message—are also important.

If you want a response of a certain type, then a choice of the right words and other communication variables that go with the words can stimulate that kind of response. In asking questions for information, sales, education, and so on, it is very important that you know how to ask.

The PAC model of the human personality allows a simple way to classify questions. When I ask a question, I speak from one ego state and direct my question at one of the other person's ego states, or perhaps at several ego states at once. For example, the verbal statement may be directed at one ego state and a non-verbal transaction may pass between two others.

All in all, as shown in Figure 7, there are nine possible simple types of transactions between ego states.

The Laws of Communication

Before getting into an analysis of questions and the procedures for gathering information, let's consider the communication laws which cover transactions between ego states.

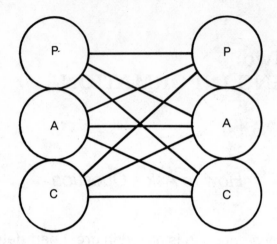

Figure 7: The Relationship Diagram

COMPLEMENTARY TRANSACTIONS

There are transactions which go between the same two ego states. Thus, if a person says, "Let me help you" (P-C), and the other replies, "Thanks, I like your help" (C-P), these are complementary transactions and can continue on indefinitely with comfort, stroking, and a desire on both sides to continue talking using these two ego states, PARENT from one person and CHILD from the other.

Another common type of complementary transaction is ADULT-ADULT:

"What time is it?"

"Three o'clock."

"How much more shall we do today?"

"I figure that I'll not be tired until 5:30."

"OK. Let's go on."

(See Figure 8.)

There are nine possible types of complementary transactions corresponding to links between three ego states as shown in Figure 7.

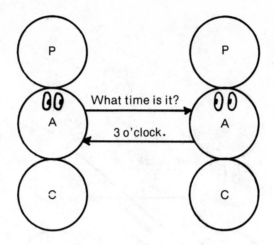

Figure 8. A Complementary Transaction

CROSSED TRANSACTIONS

Transactions may undergo a sudden switch in ego states. For example, discussion may be proceeding along on an ADULT-ADULT level when suddenly one person gets mad, switches ego states, and comes back PARENT-CHILD:

"What time is it?" (A-A)
"Three o'clock." "
"How much longer shall we work?" "
"I'm getting tired." "
"Let's work another three hours." "
(In a critical tone) "You're always pushing (P-C)
unreasonably!"

At this point, as shown in Figure 9, an ego state change occurred and the transaction became crossed. If the other person is hurt or angered, he may choose to reply from **his** PARENT and say, "You're really lazy, aren't you?" Then, the argument is off and running, and probably will end the conversation and work for the day with both sides ending up getting negative strokes.

The rule is: When transactions are crossed, communication is broken off and can only be restored by returning to complementary transaction.

35

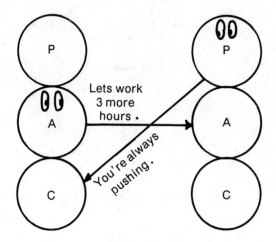

Figure 9: A Crossed Transaction

ULTERIOR TRANSACTIONS

Transactions can also be carried out at more than one level at a time. In this case one transaction is overt or obvious and the other or others are non-verbal and are transmitted via expression, tonal quality, body movement or attitude. These secret transactions or ulterior transactions can be angular—between three ego states—or parallel—between four, or even six, ego states.

The simplest type of parallel ulterior transactions is the seductive statement: (A-A) "I'll show you my etchings," which usually includes the ulterior message (C-C) "Let's get sexy." This is diagrammed in Figure 10.

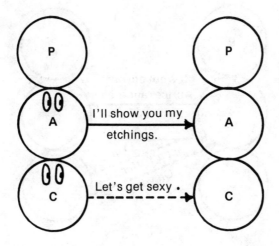

Figure 10: An Ulterior, Parallel Transaction

The salesman's ploy is a typical angular ulterior transaction. (A-A) "I think that this car is out of your price range." (A-C: ulterior) "You don't have enough money." This statement often brings the response: (A-A) "I'll buy it." (C-A: ulterior) "Oh, yeah." This transaction is diagrammed in Figure 11.

If words, combined with tone quality, facial expression, and body movement, combine to convey several messages at once, then the receiving person can easily get confused and may choose to hear one of the messages and not the others; hence, the response may be a surprise to the first speaker and may involve an ego state switch and a crossed transaction.

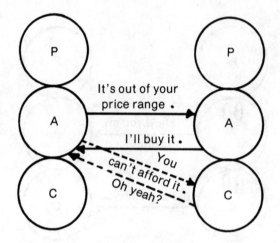

Figure 11: An Ulterior, Angular Transaction

Ulterior transactions form the basis for game playing and other destructive human interactions. A knowledge of the possibilities in human communication together with ways to sort transactions and know what messages we are sending, is very useful in enabling us to get the kind of response and strokes that we want.

Identification of Transactions and Ego States

In this section we will discuss the various types of transactions that are commonly used in communication. As non-verbal messages are difficult to put into print, we will concentrate on key types of words and phrases that can be used to identify the sending ego state and the ego state that is supposed to receive the message.

PARENT ORIGINATED QUESTIONS

The most frequent kind of PARENT originated questions are P-P and P-C. (See Figure 12.) These usually include judgmental phrases, often imply condescension, and may include polysyllabic or technical versions of equally appropriate simple words.

Some examples of P-P questions are:
1. Don't you think the quality of manufacturing is poor, compared to what it used to be?
2. Do you think he has the stuff to be successful?
3. Don't you think we'd better not invite him to the party (or into the firm): he's Irish, Black, Jewish, Catholic, Japanese?
4. How can we help him to function better?
5. Let's give her a hand—what do you say?
6. Don't you think they **should** do it this way?

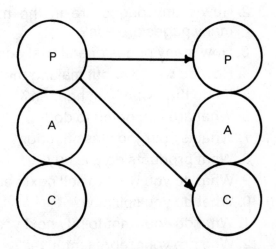

Figure 12: Most Common PARENT Originated Transactions.

Some P-C questions are:

1. How much have you accomplished today?
2. Why don't you . . . ?
3. Can I help you?
4. Why should I buy your product, advertising space?
5. How can you expect me to buy space without knowing who your readers are?

The best way to identify a P-C question is for the recipient to be aware of how he feels in hearing the question. If he feels "put down" or "one down" or scared by the question, it is likely to be a P-C.

ADULT ORIGINATED QUESTIONS

The most common and easiest to identify ADULT originated questions are ADULT-ADULT. (See Figure 13). They are usually reality-oriented and imply a "let's get on with it" attitude.

1. What time is it?
2. How many pages are in the magazine? How many pages are ads?
3. How many pages of editorial content?
4. How do we go about making these decisions?
5. If I do that, what can happen?
6. What are you going to do?
7. What is your job classification?
8. What products do you buy?
9. What do you want to sell next year?
10. What do you sell now?
11. What do you want to buy next year?
12. Who are your representatives?

A-P and A-C are harder to identify clearly and harder to state without getting mixed up with another ego state. For example, A-P: "What do you think I **should** do?" has the flavor of

C-P, and facial expression and tone of voice would be clues to which it was. A-C, "What do you really want?" has a flavor of P-C and again the tone of voices or non-verbal information could flip it one way or the other.

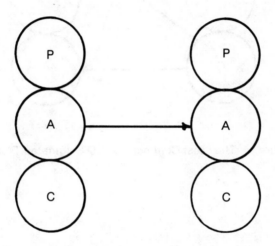

Figure 13: The Most Common ADULT Originated Transaction

CHILD ORIGINATED QUESTIONS

The most common CHILD originated verbal transmissions are C-C and C-P. (See Figure 14.) They may be full of slang, seek help or approval, or appeal to feelings.

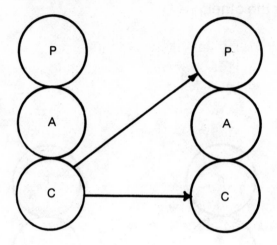

Figure 14: The Most Common CHILD Originated Transactions

C-C communications are:

1. Let's have a drink.
2. How about brainstorming this idea?
3. What's your hottest new product?
4. How can we sell a lot of these?
5. What part of your work turns you on?
6. Is your work appreciated at your lab, office, plant?
7. What do you think about this, off the top of your head?

8. How would you like to share the profits with me?
9. What do **you** think about this?

Some C-P questions are:

1. Do you like this article?
2. How can we make our magazine swing?
3. What features do you like least?
4. Why won't you buy advertising space?
5. Are we failing somewhere?
6. Should we change the design?

These are the most common and most clearly defined types of questions. More complete lists of questions, sorted by ego state, are given at the end of this chapter.

How to Use PAC Classification

If you know the ego state of the person or persons being questioned (directly or by a survey questionnaire, for example), the most suitable type of question can be selected.

It is likely that the answer you get back will come from the ego state to which you direct the question. If it comes from another ego state, you know that either you did not direct the question clearly enough or you hit a particularly sensitive area in the other personality which led to an ego state change. You then know from the response how to reaim the question. Usually one mistaken direction will not get the other person scared or angry; however, if you press this direction, chances are you will end up turning on the other's Critical PARENT state and further communication will be difficult, if not impossible.

Different groups can be expected to respond favorably to different question types. All people are likely to respond to A-A questions. In addition, there are other dimensions. For example, creative people will respond to questions directed to their CHILD. C-C is best or A-C. P-C is likely to be interpreted as a put down. Very dignified and reserved groups will probably not respond favorably to being approached in the CHILD position but would be expected to respond favorably to P-P or C-P.

43

Summary

We have now a system for classifying questions, and a system for deciding which type of questions to use for which personality and which situations.

In the following appendix are given lists of questions according to types. They are also classified according to the situation—personal or work—as different questions are more appropriate. Only a few examples are given of the personal type of questions as this manual is primarily work-oriented.

Application and Exercises

1. TRANSACTIONS

    a) List the people you communicate with most frequently.

    b) What kind of transaction do you characteristically find yourself in with these people A-A, P-P, C-C, C-P, A-P, A-C?

    c) Where PARENT ego state is involved in the transaction is it Critical PARENT or Nurturing PARENT?

    d) Where CHILD ego state is involved in the transaction is it Adapted CHILD or Natural CHILD?

    e) Which transactions are most useful? Most fun? Most uncomfortable?

2. CROSSED TRANSACTIONS

    a) For the list of people in 1(a) what kind of statements would you make in order to get a response from their Nurturing PARENT, Critical PARENT, ADULT, Adapted (Compliant or Rebellious) CHILD or Natural CHILD?

    b) Which of these statements might lead to an ego state switch and a crossed transaction?

    c) What letters or memos have you written recently from which you received unexpected or unpleasant responses?

    d) What conferences or meeting have you been at lately where you observed crossed transactions occurring?

44

3. ULTERIOR TRANSACTIONS

a) For the list of people in 1(a) what have you wanted to say and didn't?

b) In what situations do you find it necessary to cover up your true feelings, thoughts, or opinions?

c) From which people do you often receive confusing or double meaning messages, one verbally and another in between the lines by tone of voice, facial expression, or type of words used.

d) What do you think they want to say to you?

e) In what situations do you find yourself suddenly hooked into transactions different from where you started? Can you identify the ulterior or secret messages which started the switch?

4. ANALYSIS OF WRITTEN TRANSACTIONS

a) Examine several letters, memos, and so on that you have received recently. What is the general tone of the communication? Was it written by the PARENT, ADULT or CHILD?

b) If the letter has a PARENTal cast, is it Nurturing or Critical?

c) If the letter is from CHILD, is it straight or manipulative (Adapted) CHILD?

e) What does the writer say he/she wants from you? What does he really want, if this is different from the stated want?

f) Examine several letters that you have written. Analyze them according to a, b, c, d, and e above.

g) What do you want to change, if anything, about the way you communicate in writing? Which of these changes are possible without endangering your position or security or would be too threatening to those to whom you are writing?

5. ANALYSIS OF VERBAL TRANSACTIONS

a) At your next conference or meeting, identify the most used ego state of the various participants.

b) What kind of ulterior message are they sending out? How do they send the messages?

c) What are the results of the ulterior messages? What kinds of feelings are aroused in the recipients of the ulterior messages? How many crossed transactions result?

6. DESIGN OF COMMUNICATION

a) You are writing a letter, memo, or proposal or presenting a speech or a proposal to the following list of people. What distribution of transactions would you use in order to have these people be willing to listen, to understand and accept your ideas or to be most effective in reaching the goal for which your communication is directed?

	A–A	A–C	A–P	P–P	P–C	C–P	C–C
YOUR WIFE/HUSBAND	%	%	%	%	%	%	%
YOUR CHILDREN							
YOUR MOTHER/FATHER							
YOUR BOSS OR SUPERVISOR							
CHAIRMAN OF THE BOARD							
YOUR SECRETARY							
YOUR EMPLOYEES							
YOUR ASSISTANT							
YOUR COLLABORATOR							
A NEWSPAPER REPORTER							
THE PRESIDENT OF THE U.S.							
OTHERS							

REFERENCES

1. Berne, E. **Games People Play.** Grove Press, New York, 1964; (Paperback 1967). Chapter 2.

APPENDIX

PARENT to PARENT Type Questions

WORK-ORIENTED

a) Don't you think that the quality of manufactured goods is poor, compared to what it used to be?
b) How do you keep your people happy?
c) Do you think he has the stuff to be successful?
d) Don't you feel that we'd better not invite him to the party (or into the firm); after all, he's Irish (Black, Catholic, Jewish, Japanese, French, American)?
e) How can we help him to function better?
f) Don't you think they should do it this way?
g) Why don't we put our heads together on this?
h) How do you think we can show them where they stand?
i) How can we get our common values across?
j) Will you work with us to get these young companies on their feet?
k) Would you help us out by giving my staff some constructive criticism?
l) Shouldn't we work together on this project?

PERSONAL LEVEL

a) Aren't kids a mess today?
b) Don't you think that all this sex in the movies nowadays is terrible?
c) What's the best school around here for children?
d) Do you know a nice girl for my nephew to meet?
e) How can we keep these people out of our neighborhood, club, swimming pool?

PARENT to CHILD Type Questions

WORK-ORIENTED

a) Why should I buy your product or advertising space?

b) How can you expect me to buy space without knowing who your readers are?

c) Would you please return immediately the question-naire we sent you?

d) Do you want some good advice?

e) How can I support your project?

f) Why don't you be more selective in your readership?

g) Do you really have any influence in product buying?

h) What makes you think that your product is superior?

i) Do you want a special price until your company is do-ing better?

j) Can we help you with your advertising problems?

k) Can we help you with your design problems?

l) How can we assist you in maintaining and improving your product reputation?

m) Are you getting what you should from the product we sell?

n) Are you getting the response you **should** from adver-tising in our newspaper?

o) Is your product quality up to standards for advertising in our newspaper?

p) Do you really think that we are the proper magazine for your type of advertising?

q) Will you let us aid you in your advertising campaign?

r) Would you tell us what you need to facilitate your tech-nical design?

PERSONAL LEVEL

a) Why don't you . . . ?

b) Shouldn't you . . . ?

c) Can I help you?

d) Are you hungry?

e) Can't you ever do anything correctly?

ADULT to ADULT Type Questions

WORK-ORIENTED

a) What is your job classification?
b) What types of products do you buy, recommend, or design?
c) What proucts have you sold from leads via our service?
d) What do you sell now?
e) What do you intend to sell next year?
f) Who are your representatives?
g) What magazines do you read?
h) What articles do you read?
i) How many times a week are you called on by sales-men?
j) How many people use your files for reference?
k) How many of the circulation of the magazine are buy-ing influences for what we are selling?
l) Where are the buying influences?
m) Who are the buying influences?
n) When do they buy?
o) What is your company's share of the market?
p) What are recent sales and advertising trends?
q) How much time do you have to discuss this?
r) What kinds of articles that we sell are most useful to you?
s) What kinds of articles that we sell are least useful to you?
t) What kind of data is most useful to you?
u) What kind of data summaries are useful to your prod-duct design?

PERSONAL LEVEL

a) What are you going to do today?
b) What's new?
c) Did you buy the car?
d) Where is a good restaurant?
e) How much does it cost?

ADULT TO CHILD *Type Questions*

WORK-ORIENTED

a) Is this helpful to you in your design work?
b) In what ways can we work together so you can have more fun?
c) What kind of literature catches your eye?
d) How can the managers help you to enjoy your work more?
e) What gets you angry in magazine ads or writing?
f) What other procedures would make your work easier?
g) What things would increase your share of rewards in your work?
h) What kind of a gift do you want in return for filling out this questionnaire?
i) How do you want to shake up your company?
j) Are you looking for a better job?
k) What makes a job better for you?
l) What do you want from us?
m) Do you feel that our company is concerned with your problems?
n) Is our newsletter easy to read and good to look at?
o) What is the most exciting article or ad that you have seen recently in a journal?
p) What is the most exciting part of your work?
q) Which of these competing companies do you like most? Why?
r) Which of these competing companies do you like least? Why?

PERSONAL LEVEL

a) What do you really want to do?
b) Are you angry?
c) What are you feeling?
d) What do you do for fun?
e) What makes you happy?

50

CHILD to PARENT Type Questions

WORK-ORIENTED

a) Do you like this design?
b) What do you think of the editorial content of this magazine?
c) How can we improve our product?
d) What features do you like the least?
e) Why won't you buy advertising space?
f) Are we failing somewhere?
g) Should we change the style?
h) What should we charge for our product?
i) What is your best advice for us to increase our sales?
j) What kind of editorial content do you think we should concentrate on?
k) Will you give us support for this survey?
l) Will you help us establish our program?
m) Will you tell us how to best sell you our proposal?
n) Do you care if this survey is successful?
o) How can we reach the right people in this survey?
p) What can we do to satisfy you?
q) What must we do to satisfy you?
r) What is the right way to sell your product?

PERSONAL LEVEL

a) Will you help me?
b) Do you approve of me?
c) What should I do?
d) Why do you always criticize me?
e) What's for dinner?

CHILD to CHILD Type Questions

WORK-ORIENTED

a) Wouldn't it be great if our next sales meeting was in Hawaii?

51

b) How about brainstorming this idea with me?
c) What's your hottest new product?
d) How can we sell a lot of these?
e) What part of your work turns you on?
f) Do they like you at your lab, office, plant?
g) What do you think about this, off the top of your head?
h) How would you like to share the profits with me?
i) How does this strike you?
j) Are you as excited about this new feature as we are?
k) How come you don't answer our questionnaire?
l) If we give you a present, will you answer the questions?
m) How can we share the fun of your work with other engineers?
n) How much profit do you want to get?
o) Don't you like the feel of the product?
p) How can we use our plan to give you a lead over your competitors?
q) How much increase in sales do you want each year?
r) Who is the person most scared about sales in your company?

PERSONAL LEVEL
a) Do you want to play golf or chess with me?
b) Are you mad at me?
c) Do you like me?
d) Shall we go dancing?
e) Can we talk frankly?
f) Let's have a drink.

Chapter Three:
THE INTERVIEW

What's Going On Here?

In order to select a person for a particular position, type of work or type of organization, the interviewer needs information about the candidate. The validity of the information obtained will depend strongly upon the interviewer's use of his own ego states and his awareness of this use. The way the interviewer attempts to get the information he needs in order to make a decision will reflect his personality and can aid or interfere in the selection of effective staff.

The purpose of an interview is to find out about those things that the interviewee is probably afraid to tell.

Under the best, most reliable hiring conditions, the interview is only a formality. You have the candidate's record of schooling, experience, perhaps psychological testing, and letters of recommendation from people you do not know but perhaps know of. Most important of all, you have either letters of recommendation or telephone talks with one or more persons that you know and trust, who have worked closely with the individual, and who give you their clear, concise, and honest opinions.

Under these circumstances, the interview is a chance to quickly compare your personal reaction (CHILD) against the recommendation, and is not crucial. You already have enough information to make a decision. A fifteen minute interview is enough.

When the only data available is the resumé, results of testing, and letters of recommendation of doubtful validity, then the interview becomes a critical path toward the job commitment. The questions that you want answered may be uncomfortable to ask and may be threatening to answer, especially as they take place between strangers who have no reason to trust each other, or who may have the intention of manipulating each other for their own needs.

Some of the important questions are:

1. How smart are you?
2. How independent are you?
3. Can you work and share authority and decisions others?
4. What happens when you don't get your own way?
5. Can you make mistakes and take responsibility for them?
6. Have you a reasonable sex and family life that will not interfere much with the work situation?
7. Do you work hard? How lazy are you?
8. How well do you understand the work that you propose to do?
9. Do you like yourself?
10. Do you like me? Can we enjoy working to-gether?
11. What makes you angry?
12. What makes you frightened?
13. What are your strong points?
14. What are your weak points?
15. What do you really enjoy doing?
16. How much are you worth in salary?
17. Can you trust people?
18. Are you in love? With whom or what?
19. What do you want from this job?
20. What do you want from me?
21. Can you say no?
22. How do you take care of yourself?
23. What happens when you are angry, scared, or frustrated?

Classifying Interview Questions

What kind of questions are these in the PAC model? Most of the questions are CHILD-CHILD, some are ADULT-CHILD, and some are ADULT-ADULT. None in the above list are PARENT originated or PARENT directed. What questions are asked is a personal matter so some interviewers may include questions of these types. For example, some PARENT-CHILD interview questions are:

1. Why should I give you a job?
2. What can you do for our company?
3. Are you a hard worker?
4. Do you attend church regularly?
5. What is your religion?
6. Where does your family come from?
7. What did your father do?
8. Do you think that you can live up to the responsibilities of this position?
9. What salary do you expect?
10. Do you think you can come up to our standards?

Some PARENT-PARENT interview questions are:

1. How do you think we should handle this situation?
2. Will you take a firm hand when necessary?
3. Do you judge my staff to be as good as I do?
4. Do you share my prejudice on this subject?

Communication is determined by the needs and wants of both parties. What are the questions in the candidates' minds? These might be:

1. What do I have to do or say to be able to get this job?
2. How do I impress him with my ability?

3. How do I catch his interest (his CHILD)?
4. How do I avoid his prejudice, displeasure (his PARENT)?
5. What salary dare I ask for?
6. Will they like me here?
7. Will I like working here?
8. What are the future opportunities here?
9. What does he expect from me?
10. Do I dare to say what I really think?
11. Do I dare be myself here?
12. Can I compete in this company?

Fear and Trust

If both sides know what they want to ask, what prevents the interview from getting to the important questions?

The interviewer is afraid that:

1. If he starts out with straight (CHILD) questions, the interviewee will be scared and thus cautious because he will not trust the PARENT of the interviewer.
2. The interviewee will cover up any weaknesses and only talk about strengths and distort his true situation.
3. The interview will bog down to a stand off with no chance to learn what working with the person is really like (in other words, the CHILD will hide).

The interviewee is afraid that:

1. His opinions will contradict the prejudices (PARENT) of the interviewer and so his real person will not be fairly judged.
2. His ability is not sufficient and this will be discovered.
3. He will not say the right words to catch the interest (CHILD) of the interviewer and thus will not be judged to be creative and capable even though he is.

56

This is the dilemma facing both parties at the instant of the beginning of the interview. What is likely to be missing is an atmosphere of trust and a clear understanding (see p. 61, "The Interview Contract") as to how the interview will operate, in other words, what ego states will be used and how the information will be used.

Experienced interviewers have their own ways of approaching this problem and it is likely that the aim of the large majority is to establish some atmosphere of trust and comfort for the CHILD so that straight communication can take place. This may take a major part of the interview time or it may not succeed if the interviewer remains in the PARENT state. As the persons are in face-to-face contact, communication will be taking place on verbal as well as non-verbal levels and the ADULT in the CHILD, or the Little Professor, will be operating intuitively to sense all of the information coming from the other person. If the interviewer is talking CHILD and is thinking PARENT, then chances are that the interviewee will perceive this and will be getting double messages as indicated in Figure 15.

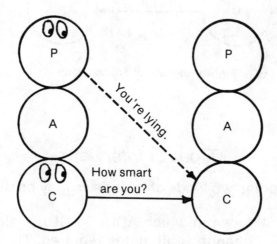

Figure 15: Angular Interview Question

The CHILD will sense the PARENT listening and judging and will be frightened and turn himself off, thus ending open communication. The most usual way of beginning to talk and establish trust is via ADULT-ADULT questions and information-giving with CHILD-CHILD transactions going on at the same time, non-verbally via facial expression, tone of voice, and general warmth of personality. This is a duplex transaction and is diagrammed in Figure 16.

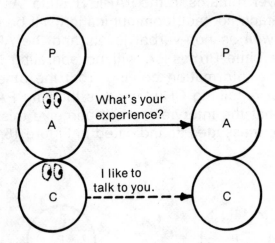

Figure 16: Parallel Transactions

Types of Interviews

At this point two kinds of interviews may be distinguished:

1. those in which ADULT-ADULT information exchange is all that is required. This is the interview for clear-cut "how to do it—can you do it" jobs such as typist, computer programmer, draftsman, machinist, in other words, jobs that involve a specific type of knowledge and not a

lot of independent decision-making and work-ing with people.

2. those in which CHILD-CHILD transactions are crucial. This involves interviews for creative, independent, decision-making, people-manag-ing positions in which the strength and aware-ness of the Little Professor (P_1) is important.

When CHILD-CHILD interaction is going on, the level of interaction is called **intimacy.** Intimacy is not limited to sexual activities of men and women, which of course is a CHILD-CHILD interaction on the C_1 or natural child level, but covers a wide range of human activity. Much of the discovery in the recent ten years of personality theory and human psychic growth has been in the area of increased knowledge and awareness of the broad-ness of the concept of intimacy.

Classes of Interview Interactions

In order to classify what goes on in human interaction and in particular in the interview, we can divide up all behavior into six classes which covers everything that man does in the time between birth and death. The classes (described in Chapter One) are: Withdrawal; Ritual; Pastimes; Activity or Work; Games; and Intimacy.

Transactions in an interview also fall into these six classes of human behavior. If the information desired from an interview of the sort aimed at by the questions on p. 54, then it will be important that at least part of the interview be at the level of **Activity** and **Intimacy.** The beginning part of the interview can comfortably be in **Ritual** and **Pastimes,** but after a few minutes these will not result in anything new being learned. **Withdrawal** of course is completely unsuitable behavior for an interview. The presence of **Games** during the interview may be useful in indicat-ing the kind of Games that the person will play after he is hired. The interviewer can make a decision as to whether this type of Game playing will interfere too much with the work to be done.

It is assumed that the interviewer is not involved in Game

playing for his own purposes. If he is, this will distort the interview and make it unlikely that sufficient ADULT information will be collected and efficiently utilized.

If the candidate is going to work closely with the interviewer and if the interviewer is a game player, then the candidate selection may depend heavily not on ADULT information and decision, but on whether the candidate will play the interviewer's Games with him.

Script Effects

As was stated earlier, human beings have a more or less rigid idea of the way their lives will go and how they will go about getting strokes for themselves depending on their early experiences in life and what they had to do (or thought they had to do) in order to get taken care of and get strokes. Games are a way of structuring time so as to get strokes and to help move life in the directions that the person expects it to go.

As a result a person will go about casting characters for his life as he expects it to be. These will usually be people who will be willing to play his Games. The more rigid the life plan or Script, the more a person is bound to play the games and find the right characters. By playing Games and getting the expected payoffs in bad feelings, the person feels that his early conclusions about life and people were justified and he feels vindicated and reinforced in his chosen life style and the associated Game playing.

Case Illustration

An industrial executive and investor had been having difficulty in finding and keeping managers and executives to work with him on various new projects. The people he hired with initial high expectations either remained too dependent on his personal decisions and/or were not willing or able to meet his standards of performance or trustworthiness.

Some early injunctions found by analyzing his life Script were: "Don't be satisfied with yourself; Don't feel your feelings; Don't trust." To the extent that these injunctions would influence his life style via

60

Critical PARENT messages, they would also be directed toward others. In order to fulfill his Script and validate these messages, he would have to intuitively hire men who would turn out to be unsatisfactory, be unable to express feelings, and be untrustworthy. In rejecting them the payoffs would be negative strokes and a feeling of justification and verification of injunctions; in other words, it's really true. "You can't be satisfied with others. Others don't express true feelings. You can't trust people."

If, after the Game is over, the conflict and bad feelings are so strong that the Game players separate, get fired or divorced, the Script-bound human will go about casting a new set of characters for the old Script and put the same old show on the road again. When he decides by himself or perhaps in counseling or therapy that the Script is a poor one and is not getting him what he wants, then he can decide to rewrite it and interact without Games, in open and parallel transactions. This decision will be reinforced if new, positive strokes are obtained in these open relationships. Positive strokes and support are crucial at these times of Script change. Why should a person give up behavior that brings him strokes—even negative—unless he gets something better in exchange? The CHILD is very practical and is always asking: "What do I have to do in order to get stroked?"

The Interview Contract

The questions on page 54 are of the types ADULT-ADULT, ADULT-CHILD and CHILD-CHILD. In order to get straight answers to these questions, an atmosphere of openness and trust must be present. I assume that it is the right of each individual to protect himself. This sometimes means lying, cheating, exaggerating, or being dishonest in a threatening situation. It is the function of the ADULT to get for the CHILD what it wants and needs. Thus a person will show one kind of behavior in the interview and after joining the organization reveal another—in unimportant ways if the interview has been an accurate one, in destructive and disappointing ways if the interview has missed vital information. The interview contract is a very important step to an

61

open and accurate interview. Like a legal contract, it must be agreed to by both parties. In the interview important points are:

1. What are we here for?
2. Is this just a formality or is it a crucial part of the application?
3. What information is needed and how will it be used?
4. If accurate information is not obtained, what are the possible consequences?

This contractual agreement which need only take a few minutes is between ADULTS; however, the approval of the CHILD is essential, and may be obtained by asking: "Is this OK with you?"

Game Effects

As there are not many Game-free adults around and as each position has its special requirements, the degree of openness, ability, independence, and creativity required is an additional ADULT input to the decision to hire or not.

It might seem advisable to match Games in an organization, in other words, if the Boss plays Game A, then his close collaborators should also. However, as the Games always end with bad feelings, this is not likely to be a stable situation. It takes two to play a Game, so if one won't play, the other cannot.

Game playing can be unlearned, so if the interviewer comes across a fine prospect in all ways except that he is a Game player, as is revealed in the interview, or is apparent in the history of his last several jobs, a possible solution is to hire him with the proviso that he attend Transactional Analysis management training, in order to attain the necessary openness and the ability to operate in a Game-free manner in the work situation.

In interviewing as well as in all life situations, it is usually helpful to be accepting of the other person and not expect perfection. If you aren't perfect, then I don't have to be, either. This can create a comfortable atmosphere in which to work and live.

Application and Exercises

1. Take a few minutes to ask yourself the question, "What do I want to learn, feel, know from an interview?" Answer from all ego states, including Critical and Nurturing PARENT, ADULT, Adapted and Natural CHILD. Check with your Little Professor on your snap judgment procedures: What do you look for instantaneously for a first impression?
2. In the first few minutes of the interview, what ego state do you usually use?
3. At what point in the interview might you experience a switch of ego states?
4. What questions do you avoid? Which ego state decides on this?
5. What feelings do you anticipate feeling near the end of a successful interview? An unsuccessful interview?
6. Classify some typical questions and statements that you might use in an interview.
   A-A
   C-C
   P-P
   P-C
   C-P
   Other
7. What kind of stroking do you use during an interview? What kind do you like to get?
8. What kind of ulterior messages do you listen for?
9. Are there any kinds of ulterior messages that you are aware of sending?
10. Aside from communication and information from other people, how do you judge the ADULT capability of the person you are interviewing?
11. How do you rate yourself on the following scale of interviewing success as measured by the performance of employees hired on the basis of your opinions?

Little success   Very successful

Little success   Very successful

12. For those employees whose success has been limited, is there any common theme or type of interaction pattern that has been involved in their lack of success?
13. What qualities, if any, do these employees have in common with present or past members of your family?
14. Do you find yourself getting involved in Game playing with these employees? Have you played these Games with your family members?
15. What are the payoffs for you in the Game playing?
16. How would you go about stopping the Games?
17. For the next several interviews you have, write down a contract as outlined on page 62 before the interview. Discuss the contract with the prospective employee. Following the interview make some decisions about the use of an interview contract in line with the following questions:
    a) If you use an interview contract, what behavior will you have to change?
    b) What kinds of risk are involved in the use of an interview contract?
    c) What feelings are aroused in you as a result of these changes?
    d) What will you get out of using an interview contract?
    e) What is your decision about your interviewing procedure?
    f) What new decisions do you want to make about it?

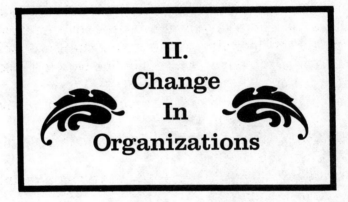

II.
Change
In
Organizations

Chapter Four:
NEEDS, WANTS, AND NEGOTIATION

The interactions that occur between management and staff can be analyzed in terms of the needs and wants of each, and what they are willing to do in order to satisfy these needs and wants. As individuals can be looked upon as being in one of three ego states, so managements can have a style that emphasizes control by PARENT, ADULT, or CHILD. This style will be set by the style of a few people high in authority or high in power, who will then assemble a management team that fits their ideas and life style.

The general rule is: People will set up their lives and populate their close environment in such a way as to maximize their comfort. Maximizing comfort usually means reducing criticism, anxiety, fear, anger, and the like, and increasing fun, play, sex, love, and similar factors. This usually involves decreasing negative stroking and increasing positive stroking. Those who cannot or will not accept positive strokes because they were trained to accept negative strokes will be more comfortable getting criticized or kicked rather than complimented. If this requires finding those who will play their Games with them, so as to get negative strokes, this will be done.

Let us first look at the needs and wants of management (considered as individuals and as the embodiment of the organization).

What Does Management Want?

▶ PROFITS. The classic goal of profit-making organizations is a return on the investment, in other word, profits. Profit is as essential to the continued existence of a self-financed organization as food, protection, and strokes are to the hu-

67

man being. Without profit, the organization must feed on itself and soon ceases to function. This money is returned to the owners of the organization and shared among the managers as a reward for positive results. Money is convertible into strokes in many ways and facilitates the procurement of food, housing, and sex—very basic wants. Money is usually a culturally (PARENT) approved commodity and so can be used in a guilt-free way to obtain pleasure. In some families, pleasure and fun may not be OK. These family members will carry the injunction, "Don't have fun," and will not be able to enjoy strokes obtained with money. Thus, there can be "rich" people who feel and act "poor" as well as "poor" people who feel and act "rich" as shown in Figure 17.

► *PUBLIC RELATIONS.* Since organizations are a part of the community, they are affected by community opinions of the organization. This is a form of recognition and, if favorable, represents positive strokes. This is also a form of self-protection as the community represents power in the political sense as well as the possibility of purchasing power. Community feelings are usually PARENT in the sense that they represent approval or disapproval from the culture. This is different from the community as purchasers or users of the product or service provided by the organization. That is a want or need and represents the public as CHILD and as the decision-making ADULT.

► *GOOD EMPLOYEE RELATIONS.* Management wants its employees to be motivated in order to be productive. It wants to be accepted by the employees in the role that it sees itself, whatever this role is—PARENT, ADULT, or CHILD. The growing effort put into employee relations is the best evidence for this want. PARENT type of management can be associated with autocratic management, while ADULT management can be associated with participative management, or management by objectives. The CHILD component of management is most important when a great deal of creativity is

68

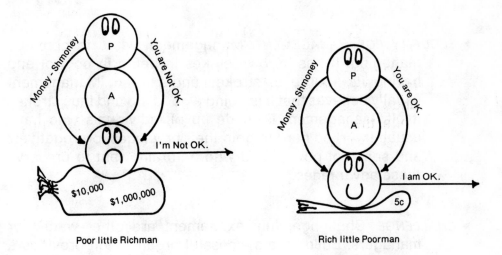

Figure 17. Richman / Poorman

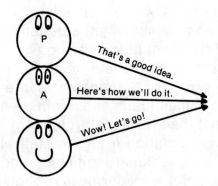

Figure 18. Power PAC.

69

required as with advertising or commercial art or with research-oriented organizations. In general, use of Critical, or even Nurturing, PARENT will turn off creative people, as the CHILD usually does not enjoy being put down and becomes angry and rebellious.

► *SECURITY FOR MANAGEMENT.* Management wants to continue managing. It has its own stakes in being in control and having its source of strokes undisturbed. Management usually believes that it is doing a good job and thus strokes itself. Management is made up of individuals who have usually worked hard to gain their privileges, prerogatives, and sense of power, and who naturally want to preserve these advantages.

► *CHALLENGE.* Challenge, fun, excitement are other wants for managers. Building a successful organization provides a feeling of OK-ness and a sense of self-actualization. This is CHILD feeling which is the most influential motivation, as the CHILD is the most powerful part of the personality and always wins out in the end. (See Figure 18.)

► *RECOGNITION FROM STAFF.* As a father gets strokes from his children, so a management can get strokes from its staff. A natural desire of human beings is to take care of other human beings and to feel needed. This is the Nurturing PARENT position. Managements are often fatherly (or motherly) to their staffs and put in great efforts to support and protect their loyal staff (children) against harm or insecurity. Recognition from the staff also gives the management an additional legitimacy and a sense of worth and leadership. A leader needs followers who will follow the leader and look up to him, in other words, parents need children.

► *RECOGNITION FROM SELF.* Just as the CHILD needs strokes from its PARENT, the management needs to feel good about

70

itself. When a person feels OK about himself, then he can go about making decisions and continue to feel OK. When he or she does not, he will be experiencing inner conflict which will interfere with ADULT functioning. So it is for management. When management does not feel that it is effective and able to make decisions, there is likely to be great conflict and confusion. Low morale is a term commonly used to describe this state. High morale involves much good feeling among staff and management about its operation and a high level of positive stroking.

► *RECOGNITION FROM THE GOVERNMENT.* Although the government in the United States is responsible to the people, the government has a PARENT position as day-to-day overseer of the economy and the operation of the various organizations in the country. As PARENT it has much power of taxation, control, criticism, or punishment for breaking its rules. Recognition from the government as a beneficial organization gives many possibilities of strokes for the organization and provides support for its functions. Many organizations need the permission of the government to operate or even to exist. If a management is the PARENT, then the government is the grandPARENT.

► *FREEDOM TO TAKE RISKS AND MAKE DECISIONS.* A principal function of management is to make decisions. Making decisions usually entails risk-taking, as the results are not completely predictable. The freedom to take risks and make decisions is not only a management need—it is a crucial key to its function. If management is locked-in to the past and cannot change, then the organization will surely be crippled and will become deadened, if not dead. As with an individual, the inability to take risks and make decisions leads to withdrawal and loss of opportunity for strokes.

► *FULFILLMENT OF OBLIGATIONS TO SOCIETY.* To the extent that organizations recognize their dependence on society and

71

accept the notion of responsibility and obligation, they develop a double view. First, they feel dependent upon the approval of society and so will work to obtain a favorable image. If this requires some special contribution to society, the management will make it, sometimes at considerable expense. Secondly, the management will adopt the feelings of responsibility that is the societal norm, and it will take the PARENT position of responsibility to those dependent upon the organization.

► *NEW IDEAS AND ENTHUSIASM.* Finally, management needs a flow of creative ideas and a fund of enthusiasm in order to carry out the work of putting these ideas into effect. Some organizations still feel that they can force or induce this flow from the PARENT position of power, and indeed, this can work for a while if the staff is dependent enough so that it has no choice but to perform, as was the case in past centuries. This approach, however, fails when the dependency no longer exists as can be seen in autocratically run families—the children leave as soon as they can.

Current management theory and practice recognize the CHILD in the form of concern for morale and motivation. The creative CHILD needs strokes in order to remain creative, an atmosphere of excitement and fun in order to retain its enthusiasm in the face of hard effort.

What Does Management Give?

►*PAYMENT.* The primary return to the staff of an organization is in the form of money. This is of primary importance because it can be converted to food, housing, and other basic needs. Money is also an aid to getting strokes, since having money means time free of work for intimacy, and the reduction of stress which interferes with intimacy. This is especially important for people who carry inner conflicts. For this reason an increase in pay, especially if it is called a merit raise, has a double stroking effect. Not only can the person buy more comfort, toys, and so on, but the notice of merit is a big stroke from the management PARENT.

► *PROMOTION, RECOGNITION, PRESTIGE.* Management has control over another set of strokes. Promotion, recognition, and prestige are powerful dimensions for external stroking and for reinforcement of internal stroking. People need to be recognized. To be ignored is very painful and can lead to the seeking of negative strokes in the form of punishment, if positive strokes are not made available. Any kind of recognition is important. This is why the appearance of employees' names in newspapers or organization communications are important. They represent strokes of recognition. A person who is stroked feels good about himself (or bad about himself if the strokes are negative). (See Figure 19.)

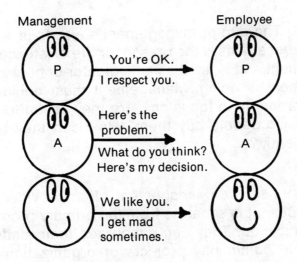

Figure 19. Management by positive stroking.

► *DISCIPLINE, PAY CUT, DEMOTION.* Pay cuts, demotions, and other types of "punishment" are used by many managements with the idea that this is an inducement to be productive. These are negative strokes. This is also the chosen approach to raising children in many families. Children who are raised in an environment where they can get only (or primarily) negative strokes will usually decide that this is the way the world is. They will set up a life style that will get for them the kind of strokes that they feel they have coming—and can get—negative strokes. This is not a comfortable way of life, but it is better than nothing. They will even turn down positive strokes and profess to prefer the negative.

Managements which are dominated by persons who have this type of life style will tend to use these methods in an attempt to motivate their staff. They will then have to pick people who expect negative strokes and hence the whole organization will develop this flavor: production amid struggle, conflict, and pain.

► *PRODUCTS.* The aim of management's efforts is some product or service. This is the reason for the existence of the management and is used as an indicator of how well the management is doing. Management must decide: What are the products to focus on? Are they useful to the community? Do people buy them? How can they be produced efficiently?

► *COMMUNITY SERVICE.* Management often provides community service that is separate from the primary products of their organization. They can encourage their staffs to participate in community projects or organizations. They can contribute money to community efforts. They can in many ways stroke the community and make their presence more welcome in this way.

► *SUPPORT, COUNSEL, ADVICE.* These are PARENT-CHILD transactions that utilize the Nurturing PARENT of the management. Support is from the Nurturing PARENT, and counsel and advice may also be nurturing although the tone may well be critical. In all relationships between human beings, this is one of the important types of transactions, provided the response is parallel CHILD-PARENT and the person being supported, counseled, or advised does not feel put down or kept in the CHILD position.

This is the way that parents as well as managements teach the lessons of tradition to the next generation. The important ingredient is how much free choice the individual has in accepting or rejecting the input from management's PARENT. Does the individual's ADULT have the autonomy to take advice or criticism from management's PARENT, pay attention to the needs and desires from his own CHILD, and then make a decision as to the best way of proceeding, in order to obtain maximum benefit for himself?

▶ *TRAINING, EDUCATION.* This is primarily an ADULT operation of management, insofar as it deals with data. Management provides more information to its staff so that it can operate with a better-equipped ADULT. Whether the staff will take advantage of this opportunity depends upon the possibilities for additional strokes. The management can have an encouraging PARENT for training and education or it can have a demanding PARENT which requires an immediate return on its investment. As training requires additional work from the CHILD, the individual will not put out the effort unless he gets something for it. Each case can be examined to see what is in it for the staff member, and the management can decide whether it is willing or capable of fulfilling the wants of the employee.

Of course some people give themselves many internal strokes for their achievements; hence, external strokes are not so critical. This life style reflects a type of early training in which the children received more positive strokes for "doing something" or "building something" or "learning something" than they received for being warm, loving, relating human beings. As a result, their life style is patterned for successively higher achievement. If this is over-intense, it may become self-defeating as successively higher achievement means harder work for the CHILD and less fun. Eventually the CHILD revolts, and may cause an ulcer, backaches, heart attacks, or other psychosomatic manifestations of inner tension.

► *LEADERSHIP, STIMULATION.* As management is naturally in a position for leadership, it can easily provide this if it knows how, and is sensitive to the difference between ADULT leadership and PARENT domination. Management can point the way and can provide long-range planning to guide the development of the organization. It can stimulate the staff to think, plan, and discipline itself to complete the work that staff and management set up.

Stimulation is felt by the CHILD. Stimulation means new possibilities for strokes, fun, excitement. As different people like different strokes, management must be careful to offer the kind of stimulation to which the CHILD will react. This quality of free choice is a characteristic of good leadership. The best followers are those who follow because they want to.

► *GROUP MEMBERSHIP.* Being a group member provides many possibilities for strokes as well as increased protection and security. Management gives group membership to its staff and can emphasize the importance of the mutual security afforded by the organization. There is a tendency for internal boundaries to form within an organization especially when it gets large or when many new employees enter. Small groups are easier to feel comfortable with than the organization at large. This, however, can cause a splitting of the organization into competing groups which may interfere with efficient operation. Management can foster this splitting into competitive groups or can encourage cross-linkage to reduce destructive competition.

76

► *CRITICISM, DOMINATION, OPPRESSION.* These are options used by the management that believes it can get best results in this way. This is the negative stroke type of management and has been justified on the basis that this is the only way to get the job done, and that the employees or slaves will not perform under any other type of management. If the employees can only accept negative strokes, then this may well be the situation. Management has more ways of giving negative strokes than it has ways, or knows ways, to give positive strokes. Thus, to use this approach is always a temptation, particularly if important members of the management became familiar with this form of behavior in their early family life. People who have been criticized, dominated, or oppressed will tend to be critical, dominating, and oppressing personalities since this was the model they could copy from their parents. (See Figure 20.)

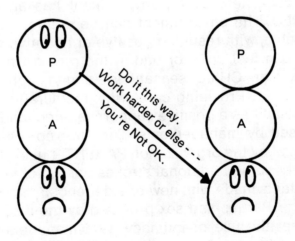

Figure 20. Management by negative stroking.

► *DECISIONS, DATA, IDEAS.* ADULT decision-making is one of the most important functions of management. Decisions, rationally and humanely arrived at, can set the stage for implementation by the staff with vigor and with a will to succeed. The management can supply much, if not all, of the data upon which it made its decisions, so that the ADULTS of the staff members can check out the calculations and decisions, and provide feedback to the management. A management with ideas will stimulate thinking and provide challenge for its staff. It is important that the ideas come from the management ADULT and are not PARENT prejudice, otherwise the staff may react via its CHILD. If they feel put down, staff members may resist change, instead of responding in the ADULT way of getting on with the job and life in general, with the maximum of comfort combined with the maximum of productivity.

► *ENVIRONMENT, FOOD, FUN, PARTIES, SEX, TRAVEL.* These are some other dimensions for stroking that the management can supply. The working environment has an effect on the CHILD. The environment can be comfortable or uncomfortable, with resulting positive or negative stroking. People can feel good or bad in the rooms where they work based on CHILD sensations—sound, light, color, odor, and view. Providing cafeterias, restaurants, or coffee for the staff has a positive supportive effect and is widely endorsed by managements. The staff not only feels taken care of by the organization PARENT, but is offered a place where some additional strokes can be obtained and new contacts made with new or old friends.

Parties and sex provided by the management represent the use of intimacy as a management tool. This offers the maximum of stroking and also the maximum risk. In this area, intimacy and Game-playing are easily confused, so it requires care to encourage true intimacy with its beneficial effects on human relationships without also encouraging sexy Game-playing with its possible destructive effects.

Travel is a bonus that management can offer to its staff. While travel can be an opportunity for change, fun, and contacting new people (which often means increased positive stroking) too much travel can simply become painful. Also, not all people are comfortable with change and new experiences, and hence will not look on travel as a source of positive strokes.

► *REJECTION.* Finally, management can provide the employee with additional proof of his Not-OK-ness by rejecting or firing him. It may be that the employee aims to prove his incapability by being fired, or it may be that he is not getting the strokes he needs and hence will not work adequately. Rejection can be made on a PARENT to CHILD level in which case the effect is most destructive. Feelings of rejection can be minimized by keeping the transaction on an ADULT-ADULT level so that the person can decide on his next move in life without feeling incapable of success.

What Does the Individual Want?

► *FOOD, FUN, SEX, PAY RAISES, PROMOTION, POWER, SELF-ACTUALI-ZATION.* These are the needs and wants of the CHILD, and the contract between management and staff is based upon them. The stroking needs for existence are sought first, then other stroking needs become important for the other motivation. The person who feels OK about himself and others and believes that he is entitled to be a winner and get many strokes everyday is the self-actualized person described by Maslow.[1] The progression of one's needs as given in Maslow's "hierarchy of needs" is: physiological (food, air, water); security (protection from physical harm); affiliation (acceptance by others); esteem (recognition by others); and self-actualization (recognition by self and decision to take responsibility for self-motivation). The last three of these categories are more clearly involved with the kinds of stroking that the CHILD seeks. As the CHILD

79

is the most powerful part of the personality, overlooking these needs can endanger the viability of the organization.

► *LEADERSHIP, DECISIONS.* Complementing the ability of management to provide leadership and decisions are the dependency needs of the staff. At the basis of these needs is the pleasure of being dependent, enjoying the CHILD position, and having someone else make the decisions and tell it what to do. Because dependency was the original position of every youngster, if the dominance experienced up to age five was not too harsh and negative-stroking or limiting, the individual can continue to enjoy and participate in this PARENT-CHILD relationship part of the time. Management's leadership and decision-making is particularly well accepted if there is also abundant ADULT-ADULT communication, so that the data can be examined and the staff can be aware of its acceptability on an ADULT basis. This is a way to stroke grownups by letting them know that they are considered to be independent human beings who can also make decisions.

► *SUPPORT, HELP, ADVICE.* Support, help, and advice provide for the dependency needs of the CHILD. These needs are particularly important in times of stress in which Not-OK feelings may surface. Many people carry some Not-OK feelings with them. When support is available in the organization though, it leaves employees in the comfortable position of children who having grown up, left the family and become independent, still enjoy being able to come home for support, advice and help when **they** choose.

► *CRITICISM, REJECTION, PERSECUTION.* When the individual wants or needs criticism, rejection, or persecution it is an indication of the adaptation of the CHILD to his early family life situation. If the only kind of attention he could get was criticism and other forms of negative strokes, including beating, then he may have adopted a life style that will

80

enable him to fulfill his needs in this way. He will reject positive strokes and expect to be negatively stroked. He will thrive on conflict. Fighting will be more exciting than intimacy. It is in this area that Games and Game-playing appear in organizations. This will be described in detail in Chapter Six. The purpose of Games and the ulterior transactions involved is to get negative strokes, to justify a chosen life position and to advance along one's Script. (See Figure 21.)

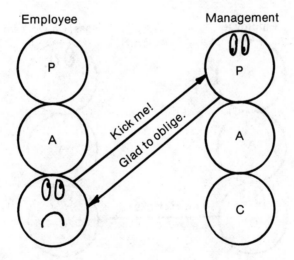

Figure 21. The need for negative strokes.

► *RECOGNITION FROM THE SUPERVISOR AND COWORKERS.* This kind of stroking is most important to the individual because it is reminiscent of the powerful influence of the parent and sister/brother positions in the families. Thus, positive strokes from the supervisor and coworkers every day are likely to create a well-satisfied, well-motivated worker. Lack of positive strokes from the boss is likely to produce an unhappy, dissatisfied, and inefficient worker. This is why supervisory time spent in talking to workers is so important. These are recognition strokes. Just the fact of saying, "I see you," is important and the time taken saying it is well spent. (See Figure 22.)

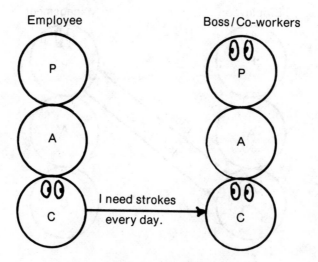

Figure 22. The basic need for strokes.

► *GROUP MEMBERSHIP.* People want to "belong." Thus, being a member of a larger group gives a feeling of security and more opportunities for stroking. Management offers a chance to belong and people want this. This is probably one of the main reasons for the growth and success of large corporations as well as for the existence of civilization—the desire to belong to a group. Groups develop behavior norms and mutual expectations that help people to predict and manifest behavior that obtains strokes.

► *TIME STRUCTURE.* A big problem to most people is what to do with their time. Work fills this need very well and supplies strokes at the same time. Most of our time between birth and death is spent in activity or work. For most people in our culture, this means working in an organization. Our cultural PARENT gives strokes of approval for accomplishments in this area. We feel good when we make or build something. When the work involves something interesting and different, this also satisfies the curiosity of the CHILD.

► *VERIFICATION OF LIFE STYLE AND LIFE POSITIONS.* As a result of early decisions, usually made before the age of five or six, individuals may have a life plan in mind based on what they think will happen to them. Depending on the severity of Script injunctions, a Script is more or less rigid. (Depending on what the punishment was, the child was more or less scared to break the rule.) The more rigid the Script is, the more difficult it is to change. The more a person is limited by his Script in his search for strokes, the more he expects and aims to obtain negative strokes at best. He will get negative strokes by getting involved in Games which have a repetitive character to them and which usually end up in bad feelings on both sides, in other words, everybody gets negative strokes. This confirms the person's Script and his expectations in life. The Scripted individual will constantly seek out those persons who will play his Games with him. He will cast his life with Script characters. He will look for work situations, bosses, management that will afford him the opportunities that he needs to get negative strokes. This then represents a want and a need for some individuals. They expect this role-playing from management. (See Figure 23.)

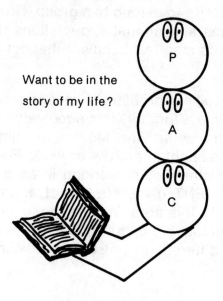

Want to be in the story of my life?

Figure 23. Life style of Script.

     In conjunction with Script decisions the person will take one of four primary life positions:

        I'm OK; You're OK.

        I'm Not-OK; You're OK.

        I'm OK; You're Not-OK.

        I'm Not-OK; You're Not-OK.

He will expect that the position that he adopts will be verified in his family, marriage, job, and life in general. A person who feels Not-OK and gets criticized on the job can take this as verification of his position and gets a certain perverse satisfaction in this verification. This will be discussed in more detail in later sections.

► *FEELING OF IMPORTANCE.* Feeling worthwhile, OK, is a very basic need for people. This is what stroking from others feels like. It is a verification of self. Each person needs to feel that he is contributing something of importance to his organization and that he is necessary to the organization. Just to be a replaceable cog is not very reassuring. In part, unions give this feeling to their members. They belong to a group which is indispensable to the organization.

► *TO BE LEFT ALONE.* Finally, individuals need some time to be by themselves, to withdraw from society and the group, and be with themselves to rest and recuperate. This may be difficult in a busy office and the availability of a quiet place is important. The ladies' room may be one such place or the coffee room another. This need to be alone is related to the individual's need to stroke himself, to be able to take care of himself, or to think.

What Can the Individual Give?

► *ENERGY, CREATIVENESS, STRENGTH.* When the potential of the creative CHILD is available through trust and stroking, then the greatest powers of the individual are at the service of the organization, group, or nation. The "I don't know" is replaced by "Let's go," and a feeling of excitement and movement is felt in the organization. This involvement of the CHILD is based on a decision by the person that he is going to get a lot of strokes and therefore is willing to put out a great deal of effort. This reservoir of strength is only imperfectly tapped in most people and represents a tremendous potential resource for any organization and management. (See Figure 24.)

► *SUPPORT, LOYALTY, COOPERATION.* As management depends upon staff effort, the support of the staff is of prime importance. The individual decides to give or not to give his loyalty, support, and cooperation. He will do this and his CHILD will concur if he expects and gets sufficient strokes

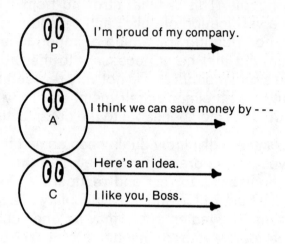

Figure 24. Staff support.

from the organization. Support, loyalty, and cooperation are based on trust between the individual and the organization, and the assumption is that the organization will respond with the same qualities in like kind.

▶ *COMPLAINTS AND CRITICISM.* If the individual is not getting enough strokes, he will probably complain at first, then will turn himself off to the organization and just do sufficient work to get by. This is one kind of complaint. Another kind is associated with a person whose complaints are part of a Game pattern designed to get him negative strokes. Here the complaints take the form of appealing to the boss as a judge against someone else. The complaints can never actually be answered as the person is not looking for a solution, but only to aggravate the boss (judge) into shutting him up. Then he can confirm his "You're Not-OK" position by saying, "They're all the same. Unfair." Encouragement will not work in this case. A Script-bound complainer can always find justification for complaints.

► *IDEAS, INGENUITY, INFORMATION.* Often the staff knows more about the day-to-day operation of the organization than the management. Hence, if they wish, the staff can be a useful source of ideas and information. The people closely associated with the details can often see room for improvements. Similarly it is easy for them to overlook problems, waste, and inefficiency if they wish. Whether the CHILD makes its ideas and ingenuity available to management depends upon the trust level and the stroking level. The CHILD will always ask, "Why should I help you? What's in it for me?"

► *COMMUNICATION, LEADERSHIP.* If the staff trusts the management and there is a good stroking system operating, then there will be good communication between the various parts of the organization. Good communication is invaluable in heading off crises and solving problems. The existence of informal organizations inside the formal organization has been discussed by Davis.[2] The informal contact structure can supply information within the organization that is not openly made available via the management. It can also help solve problems that management neglects or does not consider important enough to consider.

► *COMMUNITY CONTRIBUTION.* When the organization's image in the community is important, then the employees can contribute to this image by working on community projects. Whether a person wants to or is willing to get involved will depend upon the number and kinds of strokes available to him. If the organization recognizes community work, then employees can get strokes for their participation in it. If the person's PARENT is in favor of helping the community and neighbors, then a person will stroke himself for doing this work. Many "community contributions" are ulterior in that they can lead to making business contacts, and thus to personal profit, by knowing the right people or by having favors returned by local powers. As it is the business of each person to use his ADULT to get what his CHILD

87

wants or needs, this may cause some conflict between his own PARENT and community values of right and wrong or legal rules and laws.

▶ *FRIENDSHIP, SOCIALIZATION.* The individual can give strokes. These can range all the way from the best strokes in intimate, self-disclosing friendship, through exchanging negative strokes by Game-playing, to Pastiming strokes, strokes of recognition in working together, to ritual strokes of daily greeting and other ritualized human behavior. A management that is experiencing high or low morale in its staff is sensing the level of positive or negative stroking existing in the organization.

▶ CRITICISM. When morale is low—either because of internal conflicts of the individual or conflicts in the organization and lack of positive stroking—the CHILD will find many things to criticize. These criticisms may seemingly not have anything to do with the real problem, namely, no strokes. As the CHILD often deals in fantasy, the criticisms may not be related to reality, but may be based upon guesses and distort the true situation. The criticism will come from the PARENT because if the CHILD is too scared to reveal his true feelings, then he can call on the PARENT in his head, turn that on, and proceed to put the other person or the management down into the wrong, bad, evil, and Not-OK position. (See Figure 25.)

▶ *HARD WORK, RELIABILITY, RESPONSIBILITY.* The CHILD in the natural state wants not to have to do anything in return for satisfaction of his needs and wants. To the extent that the youngster in the early development years, up to five, had his needs filled and felt positively stroked and OK, he will be willing to negotiate with other people and agree to put off or delay some of his wants and to work in exchange for the filling of his needs and wants. It's at that point that he decides to become reliable and responsible. The degree

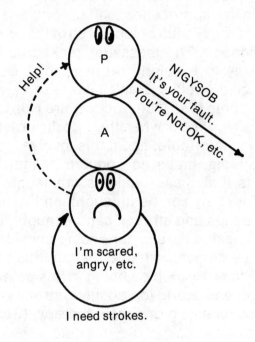

Figure 25. Covering up feelings.

to which they achieve this depends on the child and the parents. Children want to be like their parents as they are the best source of strokes. After using the parents successfully as models, the growing child can then apply this experience in the world external to its family. Their ADULT collects up this experience and reuses the procedures in order to maximize the strokes for the CHILD.

If the CHILD did not get enough positive strokes or got predominantly negative strokes, then he may believe that he cannot get positive strokes. In this case, too, the parents will be models, but the child will model their ways of getting negative strokes. This position of being Not-OK will distort and interfere with capable functioning in the working world, and will result in an inner-conflicted person experiencing various degrees of internal discomfort as he attempts to get the strokes he needs in order to exist.

89

► *SUSPICION, GREED, DISHONESTY.* Suspicion, greed, dishonesty, and similar approaches to life, work, and other people are some of the results of lack of stroking or negative stroking in childhood. The messages picked up from the parents are likely to be along the lines of: "Don't trust people. Don't give strokes. Don't take care of yourself. Parents' needs come first. Other people are Not-OK."

    People do what they do in order to make themselves comfortable, and if this involves making others uncomfortable, that's no concern of the CHILD. The main point is that these qualities are taught to children and therefore they can be untaught, and ways of getting positive feelings and strokes can be taught. Usually people in such a position are experiencing considerable pain and if it can be demonstrated to them a little at a time that they do not have to keep on being in this pain, they will want to change and work for positive strokes. This process is called counseling or psychotherapy. (See Figure 26.)

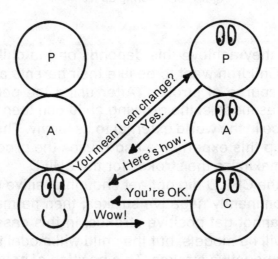

Figure 26. Permission to change.

Application and Exercises

1. In the work situation with regard to your employees or those whom you supervise, check with your ego states on the following questions:
   a) What should they do that they don't do? (PARENT)
   b) What do you want them to do that they won't do? (CHILD)
   c) What do you think it would be effective for them to do that they choose not to do? (ADULT)
2. What do your PARENT, ADULT, CHILD see as the usefulness of profits and money in general?
3. What are the most exciting (CHILD) parts of your management functions?
4. What are your duties and obligations as a manager? (PARENT)
5. In managing or manipulating those who work for you, what kinds of manipulation do you feel are OK and which ones are not OK? (Adapted CHILD)
6. In what situations do you use positive stroking to achieve your aims? In which do you use negative stroking? What success do you have with these approaches? What changes do you want to make, if any, in the use of positive stroking?
7. In what situations do you use your Nurturing PARENT? Your Critical PARENT? What are some typical statements that you use from these ego states?
8. What is your ego-gram as a manager, in other words, what is the distribution of ego state use? (Shade in as much of each column as you feel your time spent in that state warrants.)

Percent

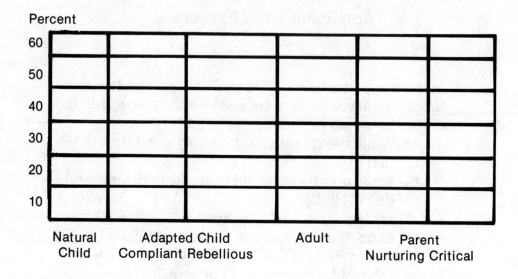

	Natural Child	Adapted Child Compliant Rebellious	Adult	Parent Nurturing Critical

9. What kind of strokes do you want from your organization? Pick four people that you know best in the organization. What kind of strokes do you think they most seek?
10. Consider your immediate superior and others to whom you are responsible. Check with each of your ego states and ask what each would like to say to these people.
11. List ten major groups to which you belong and ask yourself, "What do I want from this group? What do I get from this group?"
12. How does your role as manager help to structure your time? Make a time-structured plot around your managing time.

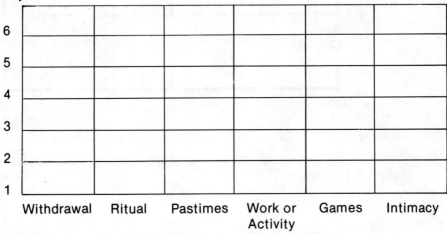

Hours Per Day

	Withdrawal	Ritual	Pastimes	Work or Activity	Games	Intimacy
6						
5						
4						
3						
2						
1						

13. Answer the questions:
   a) What did your father/mother want you to be?
   b) What did other influential people in your life want you to be?
   c) Name some people that you most admire in present or past history.
   d) What kind of books did you like to read when you were little?
   e) How do the answers to questions (a) through (d) fit in with the position you find yourself in now?

14. What are the strong points and weak points of your creative CHILD (as estimated by your ADULT and Critical PARENT)? How do these views differ? Which view do you usually listen to?

15. Locate yourself in your organization on the following scales.

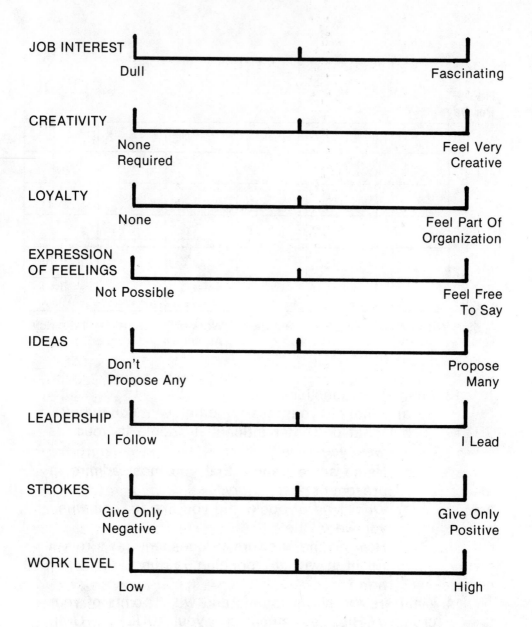

JOB INTEREST
Dull   Fascinating

CREATIVITY
None   Feel Very
Required   Creative

LOYALTY
None   Feel Part Of
                                        Organization

EXPRESSION
OF FEELINGS
Not Possible   Feel Free
                                        To Say

IDEAS
Don't   Propose
Propose Any   Many

LEADERSHIP
I Follow   I Lead

STROKES
Give Only   Give Only
Negative   Positive

WORK LEVEL
Low   High

1. Maslow, A. **Motivation and Personality,** Harper & Row, New York, 1954.
2. Davis, K. **Human Relations at Work,** McGraw Hill, New York, 1967, Chapter 13.

Chapter Five:
THE EFFECTS OF MANAGEMENT STYLE

*Analysis of Styles by Using Different,
Current Management Models and PAC*

The variety of leadership, management, and organizational styles can be examined and classified using the PAC personality model. At this point the division between system and individual begins to come into focus. Do we have to make a choice between the system and individual approach? PAC is an individual approach. If we understand the dynamics of an individual or perhaps a few important individuals in an organization, can we understand and predict organizational behavior? Are there other variables that we will not be able to discover by looking at individuals and therefore we must look also at the system as a whole?

In the sciences of physics, chemistry, and especially biology, this problem is a very old one. Scientists believe that if they could understand the fundamental forces and laws of nature, then they could, by the use of mathematical models, correlate and predict the results of all future measurements on any physical system. These predictions turn out to be, however, statistical predictions. The problem with describing a large system via a mathematical model lies in the difficulty in describing all of the complexities, even though all of the basic laws may be known. This is where system theory becomes useful. A whole section of the world can be considered as a unit, a black box, its properties described, and its response measured without having to consider the details of what is going on inside.

In an organization, this can be translated in the following terms: if an organization is small, then its operation is determined by the behavior of relatively few people. Their personalities and management styles determine the operation of the organization.

The communication lines are small in number so that the process of information transfer can be clearly followed and changed if desired.

When an organization gets large, say more than a thousand people, then the power begins to get diffused, because no one person can keep close enough touch with all of the decision making and the other necessary operational details. Much authority must be delegated; an informal organization begins to grow to complement the communication channels of the formal organization. It becomes difficult to know all of the sources of input that influence decisions. At this point, it becomes useful to go over to the systems approach and consider the organization as a set of subsystems, and by attempting to understand and develop empirical rules for the behavior of these systems, to understand and predict the behavior of the organization.

Let's look at several organizational theories in current use.

THEORY X AND THEORY Y

The Theory X-Theory Y approach to management, as described by Douglas McGregor,[1] can be analyzed from the lists of assumptions each management style is based on:

THEORY X
1. Work is inherently distasteful to most people.
2. Most people are not ambitious, have little desire for responsibility, and prefer to be directed.
3. Most people have little capacity for creativity in solving organizational problems.
4. Motivation occurs only at the physiological and security levels.
5. Most people must be closely controlled and often coerced to achieve organizational objectives.

THEORY Y
1. Work is as natural as play, if the conditions are favorable.
2. Self-control is often indispensible in achieving organizational gains.
3. The capacity for creativity in solving organizational problems is widely distributed in the population.
4. Motivation occurs at the affiliation, esteem, and self-actualization levels as well as physiological and security levels.
5. People can be self-directed and creative at work if properly directed.

Among the list of Theory X assumptions, all but number four are clearly judgmental and prejudiced; thus, they belong to the Critical PARENT. Theory Y assumptions are ADULT statements with a lot of CHILD feeling implied in statements one and three. The Theory X position is "They're Not-OK." Stroking and resulting motivation come only externally and negative stroking is seen to be motivating. Theory Y takes the position "They're OK," and that people are motivated by self-stroking and self-esteem, in addition to external stroking. Negative stroking is not considered to be motivating. (See Figure 27.)

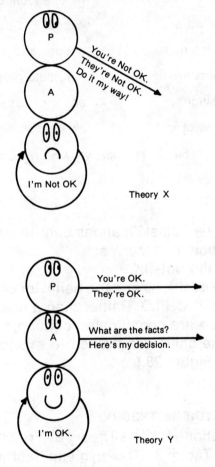

Figure 27. McGregor's Theory X and Theory Y type managers.

IMMATURITY-MATURITY THEORY

Chris Argyris's immaturity-maturity theory[2] is exemplified in Table 2.

IMMATURITY	MATURITY
passivity	increased activity
dependence	independence
behave in a few ways	capable of behaving in many ways
erratic shallow interests	deeper and stronger interests
short time perspective	long time perspective (past and future)
subordinate position	equal or superordinate position
lack of awareness of self	awareness and control over self

Table 2: *Immaturity-Maturity Continuum*

These two classifications can be summarized as the way people feel about themselves:

I'm Not-OK.   I'm OK.

These are the positions and the behavior of people with a Not-OK CHILD or an OK CHILD. Rather than a measure of immaturity or maturity, which are complicated concepts, these are a measure of whether the child was trained to expect negative or positive strokes. (See Figure 28.)

MOTIVATION-HYGIENE THEORY

Motivation-Hygiene Theory by Frederick Herzberg[3] is characterized in Table 3. The hygiene factors serve primarily to prevent job dissatisfaction while the motivators are effective in attaining superior performance. This can be looked at in terms of the stroking levels. The motivators are clearly better sources of positive strokes. Also, the motivators are more clearly directed

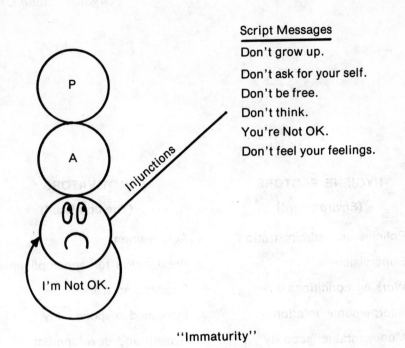

Script Messages

Don't grow up.

Don't ask for your self.

Don't be free.

Don't think.

You're Not OK.

Don't feel your feelings.

Injunctions

I'm Not OK.

"Immaturity"

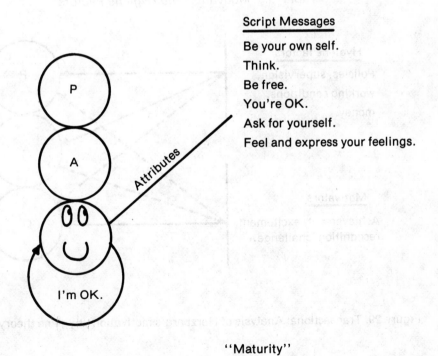

Script Messages

Be your own self.

Think.

Be free.

You're OK.

Ask for yourself.

Feel and express your feelings.

Attributes

I'm OK.

"Maturity"

Figure 28. Argyris Immaturity - maturity theory in TA script language.

HYGIENE FACTORS (Environment)	**MOTIVATORS** (The Job Itself)
Policies and administration	Achievement
Supervision	Recognition for accomplishment
Working conditions	Challenging work
Interpersonal relations	Increased responsibility
Money, status, security	Growth and development

Table 3: Motivation and Hygiene Factors

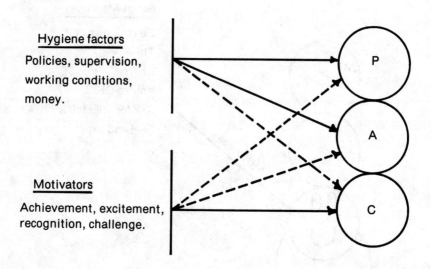

Figure 29. Transactional Analysis of Herzberg's motivation - hygiene theory.

at the CHILD ego state, the source of power in the personality. The motivators are in language that the CHILD understands. They refer to excitement, creativity, freedom of choice, and strokes. The hygiene factors can be applied in an ADULT or PARENTal way and are not so clearly connected with positive strokes. (See Figure 29.)

MANAGEMENT SYSTEMS

The four types of management systems described by Rensis Likert[4] range from a task-oriented, highly-structured authoritarian management style to a relationships-oriented style based on trust, teamwork, and confidence. The description utilizes twenty items. Some examples are:

1. The extent to which superiors have confidence and trust in subordinates.
2. The manner in which motives are used.
3. The amount and character of interaction.

The scales on these items go from fear, distrust, punishment, and withdrawal, to trust, economic rewards, participation, goal-setting, and friendly (intimate) interaction.

Clearly, the scale is one of stroking from negative to positive, and the presence of injunctions from the management, such as "Don't trust," "Be scared," "Don't have fun," "Don't stroke."

This management systems or leadership style approach to the behavior of organizations has been considered by a number of other groups. The Ohio State leadership studies[5] focus down to two dimensions: initiating structure and consideration, which refer to task-oriented and relationships-oriented management dimensions.

Initiating structure refers to "the leader's behavior in delineating the relationship between himself and members of the work-group and in endeavoring to establish well-defined patterns of organization, channels of communication and methods of procedure"—task oriented.

Consideration refers to "behavior indicative of friendship, mutual trust, respect, and warmth in the relationship between the leader and the members of his staff"—relationships oriented.

101

The University of Michigan Survey Research Center studies[6] resulted in the defining of two dimensions which they called production-orientation and employee-orientation similar to the above. Cartwright and Zander, from findings at the Research Center for Group Dynamics, discuss all group objectives in terms of two categories: the achievement of some specific group goal and the maintenance or strengthening of the group itself.[7] Again, these connect to task and relationship dimensions.

THE MANAGERIAL GRID

The Managerial Grid leadership styles were developed by Blake and Mouton.[8] The five leadership styles that they describe —impoverished, country club, task, middle-of-the-road, and team —are shown on Figure 30 below. These cover management's focus and way of dealing with employees.

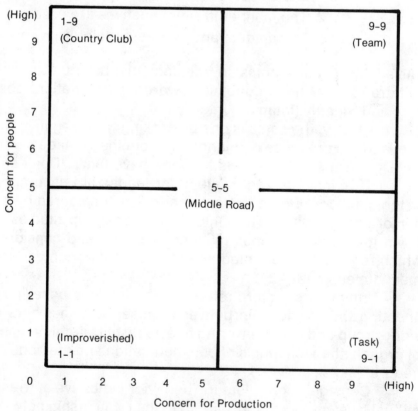

Figure 30: The Managerial Grid Leadership Styles

An additional dimension to these has been contributed by Hersey and Blanchard.[9] This reflects the reality that any of these four leadership styles can be effective or ineffective in organizational life. They define the two management grid dimnsions in terms of task and relationship measures, and add a dimension of effectiveness. This dimension was first considered by William Reddin.[10] The resulting management space is shown in Figure 31.

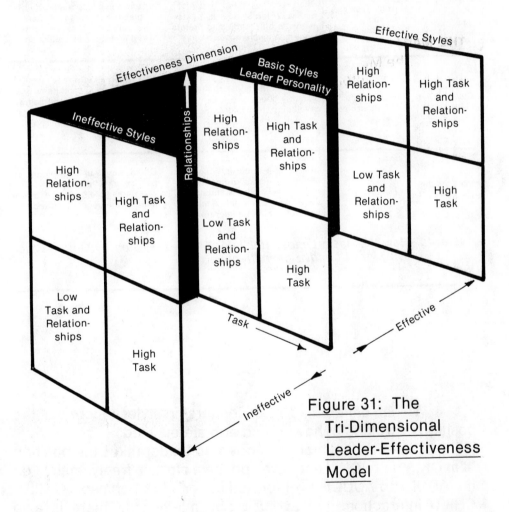

Figure 31: The Tri-Dimensional Leader-Effectiveness Model

Table 4 gives some brief descriptions of the leadership styles described by this effectiveness model. The correspondence to the managerial grid is also indicated.

Managerial Grid	Tri-Dimensional Basic Styles	Effective	Ineffective
Task (9-1)	High Task	Often seen as knowing what he wants and imposing his methods for accomplishing this without creating resentment.	Often seen as having no confidence in others, unpleasant, and interested only in short-run output.
Team (9-9)	High Task and Relationships	Often seen as a good motivator who sets high standards, treats everyone differently, and prefers team management.	Often seen as a person who tries to please everyone and, therefore, vacillates back and forth to avoid pressures in a situation.
Country Club (1-9)	High Relationships	Often seen as having implicit trust in people and as being primarily concerned with developing their talents.	Often seen as primarily interested in harmony and being seen as "a good person," and being unwilling to risk disruption of a relationship to accomplish a task.
Impoverished (1-1)	Low Task and Low Relationships	Often seen as appropriately permitting his subordinates to decide how the work should be done and playing only a minor part in their social interaction.	Often seen as uninvolved and passive, as a "paper shuffler," who cares little about the task at hand or the people involved.

Table 4:   *How the Basic Leader Behavior Styles are Seen by Others When They Are Effective or Ineffective*

We can understand these leadership styles in terms of the positions, stroking behavior, and ego states used.

The effective, high task-oriented leader takes the position "I'm OK, You're OK," and gives positive strokes freely, mainly on the ADULT to ADULT level for activity or work behavior. CHILD-CHILD interactions are avoided and minimized. There is also authoritative PARENT to CHILD transaction and the expected CHILD anger is minimized by the use of considerable supportive PARENT to CHILD stroking.

The ineffective, high-task oriented leader takes the position "I'm OK, You're Not-OK" and gives more negative than positive strokes; he operates mainly on the PARENT-CHILD levels.

The effective high task and relationships style leader takes the position "I'm OK, You're OK," giving positive strokes freely on the ADULT-ADULT level for activity or work behavior and also on the CHILD-CHILD level on an intimacy or relationship basis. (See Figure 32.)

The ineffective high task and relationships leader takes the position "I'm Not-OK, You're OK"; he offers strokes from his CHILD and operates mainly with CHILD to PARENT transactions. He is likely to turn on Critical PARENT (when his CHILD gets scared or angry) with negative stroking and resultant demotivation.

The effective high relationships leader takes the position "I'm OK, You're OK"; he strokes freely on a CHILD-CHILD level, and is more concerned with intimacy level behavior than with activity or work behavior, and less with ADULT-ADULT transactions which are concerned with productivity and decision making.

The ineffective high relationships leader operates from the "I'm Not-OK, You're OK" position; he offers positive strokes freely and he needs positive strokes. He avoids ADULT-ADULT confrontation which may risk anger and conflict. He avoids stating PARENTal expectation and values and neglects or avoids ADULT decision-making. As a result the staff feels OK as it is and is not motivated toward a set of goals essential for the organization's existence.

The effective low task and relationships leader takes the "I'm OK, You're OK" position. He offers positive strokes freely to his staff for taking responsibility for work and getting strokes for themselves. His relationships are on an ADULT-ADULT level with very little direct CHILD-CHILD interaction.

The ineffective low task and relationships leader has taken the position "I'm Not-OK, You're Not-OK" and characteristically is in the withdrawn position. He does not give or get many strokes and the few that are exchanged are mostly negative. His relationships are on the CHILD-ADULT or CHILD-PARENT levels with his CHILD in the Not-OK position. (See Figure 33.)

105

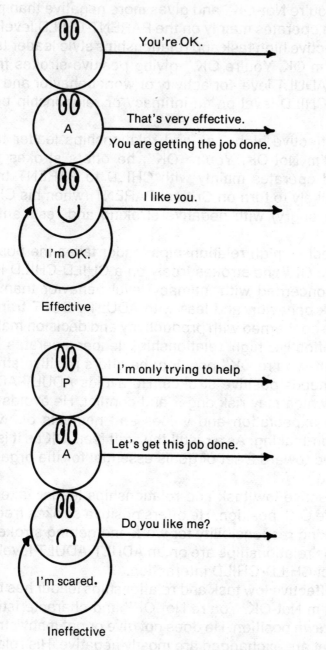

You're OK.

That's very effective.

You are getting the job done.

I like you.

I'm OK.

Effective

I'm only trying to help

Let's get this job done.

Do you like me?

I'm scared.

Ineffective

Figure 32. High Task and Relationships leaders.

106

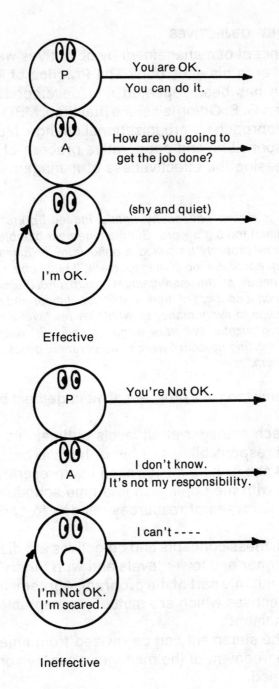

You are OK.
You can do it.

How are you going to
get the job done?

(shy and quiet)

I'm OK.

Effective

You're Not OK.

I don't know.
It's not my responsibility.

I can't - - - -

I'm Not OK.
I'm scared.

Ineffective

Figure 33. Low Task and Relationships Leader.

MANAGEMENT BY OBJECTIVES

The concept of management by objectives was described by Peter Drucker in his early book **The Practice of Management** and the theme has been repeated and developed by him[11] and others including G. S. Odiorne[12] since that time. MBO has become an important approach for organizational change. MBO proposes a creative, responsible, and cooperative process of goal setting aimed at increasing the effectiveness of management. To quote Drucker:[11]

> "I do not use the word 'philosophy' lightly; indeed I prefer not to use it at all; it's much too big a word. But management by objectives and self control may properly be called a philosophy of management. It rests on a concept of the job of management. It rests on an analysis of the specific needs of the management group and the obstacles it faces. It rests on a concept of human action, behavior and motivation. Finally, it applies to every manager, whatever his level and function, and to any organization whether large or small. It insures performance by converting objective needs into personal goals. And this is genuine freedom."

The basic steps in a program of management by objectives are as follows:

First, each manager at all levels outlines his concepts of the duties and responsibilities of his or her job and a list of the objectives that she or he aims to reach in a prescribed period of time. Included with the objectives is a time schedule and a listing of the various types of resources needed to carry out these objectives.

Second, these concepts and objectives are discussed with managers at higher and lower levels and with others who are interconnected with this part of the program. Agreement is reached on a set of objectives which are mutually acceptable. The result is a written statement.

Third, the statement can be revised from time to time but only with the agreement of the manager's supervisor and others closely concerned.

Fourth, there is periodic evaluation of progress toward and achievement of the objectives set. These evaluations may take the form of reports, meetings, and so on.

This system is clearly meant to be an ADULT programed approach to getting things done. Drucker in the statement quoted above refers to the concepts of human motivation and personal goals and so implies paying attention also to CHILD needs and wants as well as to the PARENT values and definition of freedom. This view of problem solving points up the advantages of MBO as well as the potential weaknesses.

If the managers at the various levels can truly take part in the setting of objectives, and can get objectives accepted that take into account the manager's internal CHILD needs for creativity and stroking, then we would have the highly desirable condition of the ADULT listening to the CHILD and working together with the CHILD to get its needs met. This is the optimum condition for the unleashing of the power of the CHILD for problem solving and fulfillment of objectives.

If, however, the MBO process is a thinly (or thickly) disguised Critical PARENT operation for exploitation of the manager's CHILD, then the organization is no better off than with an open Theory X type management. In this case the management will probably be operating from a PARENT contaminated ADULT. "You had a free choice in setting these objectives, so what are you complaining about now?" Chances are that the choice was not so free but was made under more or less subtle pressure from the supervisor. The MBO structure, then, needs some ways to confront these destructive processes by the safe expression of fears and resentments.

Also, once the objectives have been set, not enough attention is usually paid to the question of motivation. Why should the CHILD turn its energies towards the fulfillment of the objectives? Do the manager's personal needs also have a place in the planning process? If not, and if personal needs are expected to be continually kept at lower priority with regard to organizational needs, then the situation has been set up for Game playing, blaming, and demotivation of the CHILD.

These problems of motivation in the MBO process have been discussed by Batten[13] in his book **Beyond Management by Objectives.** Batten's ideas fit in well with the TA idea of the need for high stroking levels as a motivater.

Thus management by objectives can at best be a highly

109

effective way to increase the effectiveness of managers and at worst can be another conspicuous failure in the long chain of management theories. This will depend upon whether the ego states involved are the free and creative CHILD, the ADULT and the Nurturing and Protective PARENT or the Critical PARENT and Adapted CHILD.

Ego States and Management Style

In this section we will discuss the effects of various ego states on management style. A leader may be operating predominantly out of a single ego state, two ego states, or out of all three ego states interchangeably. He may be operating out of overlapping or contaminated ego states. Each of these situations will have characteristic effects on his style, and the effects he has on his staff or group.

INFLUENCING OR CRITICAL PARENT

The influencing or Critical PARENT comes across as domineering, insisting, never satisfied, suspicious, demanding, and exacting. Transactions are felt as negative stroking. In an organization in which Critical PARENT is dominant, the atmosphere will be one of mistrust, suspicion, lack of privacy, high pressure, and high tension. The safest position to take in this organization is Adapted CHILD: to do what one is told to do and not talk back, to suffer in silence. ADULT will be difficult to maintain as there will be very little positive stroking. ADULT functioning is dependent on the CHILD staying quiet. If the CHILD feels deprived, bored, angry, or hurt then as CHILD is a more powerful ego state, it can take over control of the personality. It takes considerable energy for a person to remain ADULT when his CHILD is acting up. If the CHILD is getting strokes then it will allow the ADULT to function. (See Figure 34.)

As a family can be characterized by the type of stroking available, so in an organization in which negative stroking predominates, the staff will develop its own methods for adapting and manipulating the organization in order to obtain the strokes

110

and security that it needs. The style will tend to be self-perpetuating as this type of organization will attract staff who have been used to taking an Adapted CHILD position with their own Critical PARENTS. Eventually these people become part of the management and as they carry the Critical PARENT in their own heads, they can easily become in turn domineering, critical, and so on, and thus continue the sequence.

SUPPORTING PARENT

The effect of the supporting PARENT in management style is seen primarily in the fringe benefits, security provisions, pension plans, and other employee services which have to do with the maintenance needs of the staff. The supporting PARENT is most concerned with the hygiene factors described by Herzberg. The welfare of the CHILD is of prime importance. Lack of concern for these needs can hurt morale, in other words, feelings of safety and security. However, concern for these needs does not necessarily motivate employees. Supporting PARENT is an important ingredient of any relationship and in a reasonable proportion provides a great deal of warmth and comfort to relationships which exist amidst the conflict and difficulties of living. Over-support can encourage and stroke the continuation of Games such as "Poor Me," "I Was Only Trying to Help," and others.*

ADULT

ADULT is the reality-testing, data-handling, decision-making part of the personality. An organization without a good functioning ADULT will not live long in the competitive world. An organization must always be making decisions as to the best ways to continue its existence and to obtain what it needs and wants for its investors, owners, staff, management, and so on. It must do this amidst the sometimes conflicting desires of the CHILD needs and wants, and the PARENT-seen duties, obligations, principles of the management, and the culture in which the organization lives and from which it derives its support.

* See further discussion of Games in Chapter Six, following, and in *Games People Play* by Eric Berne.

It is the job of the ADULT to listen to both PARENT and CHILD input and make decisions about the best directions to go. The strength of the collective ADULT in an organization can best be seen in times of crisis. The organization can then switch to one of three modes. It can become PARENT: defensive, attacking, relying on past procedures and operations, and rigid. It can become CHILD: scared, indecisive, withdrawing, giving up, running away, or operating in fantasy with high risk projects. Or, it can turn on its ADULT, take a good hard look at the facts and begin to plan getting on with life in the changed circumstances in which it finds itself. The ADULT in the organization will have to take into account the feelings and commands coming from the PARENT and CHILD ego states; to ignore these is likely to result in internal sabotage in one way or another. The ADULT can make contracts and decisions; however, without the power and enthusiasm of the CHILD to validate the contract, the organization cannot carry out its contracts.

OK CHILD

An organization with an OK CHILD can be heard and felt. This may occur in the entire organization, or in one part, one section, one floor, or one office. When the OK CHILD is allowed and encouraged, there will be a lot of positive stroking. As a result the noise level will be higher. People will be more alert and inventive. The organization will experience the elements commonly lumped under "high morale." There will be much social activity, much concern for the welfare of the group and the organization. Loyalty, hard work, and high motivation are the results of a situation where positive stroking is encouraged and freely exchanged between management and staff. This does not mean phony strokes. The CHILD is very sensitive to double messages and will detect manipulative strokes. The presence of OK CHILD in an organization will be highly correlated with the absence of Critical PARENT. Decisive ADULT will be accepted if the stroking level is adequate.

NOT-OK CHILD

This collective ego state in an organization or part of an

organization shows itself in the levels of fear, anxiety, and compliance, and in the presence of indirect maneuvers to get strokes which are likely to be negative. Because a Not-OK CHILD is a result of children adapting to their parents and family at an early age, a management is not likely to be the **cause** of Not-OK feeling. In the presence of an extremely critical, demanding, and harsh PARENT, such as exists in some political systems or illegal organizations in which the rule is actually adapt or die, the Not-OK feelings can be "brainwashed" into the psyche at any age.

In the usual organization with a strong, autocratic management system, the effect would be to stroke the staff for their Not-OK feelings. This would accentuate the Not-OKness. Also, the personnel practices would be influenced in such a way that personnel would be hired who were judged, perhaps in non-verbal ways, to carry a Not-OK CHILD. This would populate the staff with fearful and adaptable people with the result that the organization could be characterized as having a Not-OK CHILD. (See Figure 34.)

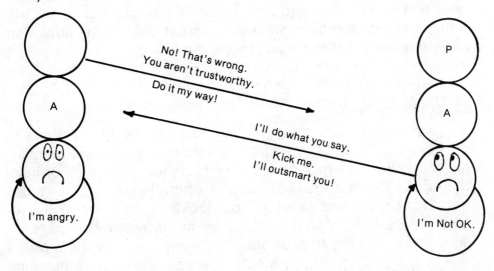

Management by Critical PARENT

The Not-OK, Adapted Child Staff

Figure 34 Management by Critical or Influencing PARENT.

Excluded and Excluding Ego States

As there can be exclusion of one or more ego states or contamination of one ego state by another in an individual, so these conditions can also be seen in organizations. Their presence is dictated by these conditions in the individual staff members and accentuated by hiring practices.

EXCLUDED ADULT

When ADULT operation is not allowed or encouraged in an organization, management will be predominantly PARENTal, either autocratic or benevolent, combined with a lot of Adapted CHILD, either Compliant or Rebellious. Management will operate the way it has always operated because that's the way it has always been! New ideas and change are strongly resisted; there may be a traditional father and child relationship between the boss and the employees. Planning for change will be at a minimum and there is likely to be a great deal of conflict within the management, open or secret, and a great deal of manipulation and secret negotiation to get around the rules.

EXCLUDED PARENT

PARENT has two aspects. It carries the connections to past experience as learned from others and is thus available for instant decisions which do not have to be reasoned out nor have the odds calculated as with ADULT operation. Some examples are "Don't cross the street without looking!" or "Don't kill people!" PARENT can come across as nurturing, taking care of, supportive, and the like, or critical, demanding, insistent, prejudiced, and the like. When PARENT messages are overdemanding or overthreatening, the person may exclude the PARENT completely and thus eliminate all dependence on cultural and moral values.

Management without any PARENT can be on the psychopathic side of illegality, criminality, and in general, disregard for any values except its own desires for what it wants for itself. The ADULT is without the use of the PARENTal checks and balances.

EXCLUDED CHILD

In an organization where CHILD is excluded, creativity, new ideas, enjoyment of work or human relationships is minimized. The organization is run from an autocratic point of view using the past as a reference point, with a strict eye for results based on PARENTal values and ADULT objectives and small concern for stroking needs of the CHILD. As the excluded CHILD is a very powerful force and will attempt to intrude in order to get its needs met, this is at best an unstable situation which ends in self-destruction, continual escalation of PARENTal control, revolution, or rebellion.

EXCLUDING EGO STATES

Another set of behavior patterns in organizations can be seen if one type of ego state dominates the organization management. An overly PARENTal type of management can produce an autocratic type of organization or one of a benevolent PARENT type of family organization. An overly ADULT type of management will lead the organization toward ever-expanding goals, profits, and so on, without concern for the values of the culture or without regard for the human needs of the CHILD. The excluded CHILD will make his presence known to the executives in this organization in the form of ulcers, migraine headaches, back trouble, heart attacks, and other psychosomatic symptoms of the deprived CHILD.

A management that is heavily CHILD dominated may be very creative and operate without close contact with reality and thus go bankrupt as a result of too much fantasy about the way the real world operates. Ignoring of cost control is a typical symptom of dominant CHILD. (See Figure 35.)

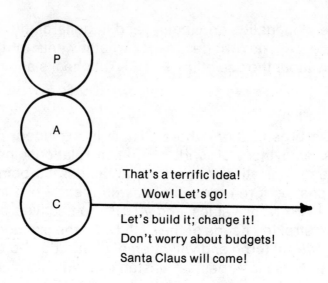

Figure 33. Management by CHILD.

Application and Exercises

1. Check your managerial styles with the following questions:
   a) How do you feel about yourself? OK? Not-OK? In what ratio?
   b) In what ways are those you supervise OK? Not-OK?
   c) How do you use your PARENT in managing? Your ADULT? Your CHILD?
   d) Consider a decision you are involved in making now. How are you utilizing your various ego states in making this decision? Which ego state do you use to communicate your decision to your staff?
   e) What does your PARENT say about work? About play and fun?

2. What are the **Don't** messages in your head that might have an effect on your managing style? The **Do** messages or **Be** messages that have an effect?
3. What ways have you adapted to **Don't** messages that you would like to change? How will you go about this change?
4. Examine the basic styles given in Table 4. Make up a standard diagram such as shown in Figures 32 and 33 with PARENT, ADULT and CHILD messages that describe your feelings, thoughts, and opinions as a manager.
5. Consider the following set of ego states operating in your fellow managers. What messages, verbal or non-verbal, do you hear, see, or feel are being sent?
   a) Critical or Protecting PARENT
   b) Nurturing or Rescuing PARENT
   c) ADULT
   d) Adapted (Compliant or Rebellious) CHILD
   e) Natural or Creative CHILD
6. Which managers do you see who have excluded one ego state or operate mainly from one ego state? How does this affect their managerial style? Their goal-achieving ability? Their relationship with superiors, colleagues, and subordinates?

REFERENCES

1. McGregor, D. **The Human Side of Enterprise,** McGraw Hill, New York, 1960.
2. Argyris, C. **Integrating the Individual and the Organization,** Wiley, New York, 1964.
3. Herzberg, F. **Work and the Nature of Man,** World Publishing Co., New York, 1966.
4. Likert, R. **The Human Organization,** McGraw Hill, New York, 1967.
5. Stogdill, R. and Coons, W. (eds.) **Leader Behavior: Its Description and Measurement,** Research Monograph #88 (Columbus, Ohio: Bureau of Business Research, Ohio State University, 1957).

6. Katz, D., Maccoby, N. and Morse, N. **Productivity, Supervision and Morale in an Office Situation,** Darel Press, Detroit, 1950.
7. Cartwright, D. and Zander, A. **Group Dynamics: Research and Theory,** Row Peterson, Evanston, 1960.
8. Blake, R. and Mouton, J. **The Managerial Grid,** Gulf Publishing, Houston, 1964.
9. Hersey, P. and Blanchard, K. **Management of Organizational Behavior,** Prentice Hall, New Jersey, 1969.
10. Redding, W. "The 3D Management Style Theory," **Training and Development Journal,** Apr. 1967.
11. Drucker, Peter F. **The Practice of Management,** Harper and Row, New York, 1954, pp. 121–136.
12. Odiorne, G. S. **Management Tasks, Responsibilities, Practices,** Harper and Row, New York, 1973, pp. 430–442.
    ————. **Management by Objectives,** Pitman Publishing Company, New York, 1965.
13. Batten, J. D. **Beyond Management by Objectives,** American Management Association, Inc., New York, 1966.

Chapter Six:
GAMES PLAYED IN ORGANIZATIONS

Why People Play Games

Games were discussed briefly in Chapter One. In this chapter Games that especially apply to organizations will be discussed. These and many Games in the TA sense have been analyzed in detail in books which can be found among the references at the end of Chapter One. Game analysis is useful in identifying Games and this is the first step toward stopping these transactions and their usually destructive results.

In the search for strokes people develop their own unique ways of getting what they want and need. If, during early family life, this need for strokes is frustrated and the CHILD invents devious ways of getting strokes (usually negative strokes since he believes negative strokes are the only kind available), the individual has learned to play Games. Games played in life outside the family, and thus, in organizations were first taught to the children in the family. Games are meant to end with each side collecting negative strokes as a payoff. The bad feelings can be saved up as "brown stamps," collected in order to be cashed in at a later time as justification for a "guilt-free" rage, tantrum, week-end drinking binge, job quitting, divorce, or suicide. The aim of Games is to confirm for the person that the world and other people are really what he decided they were when he was young, and that his life style was therefore chosen correctly. Each time the Game is played the Script is advanced toward its anticipated end. Failure, getting nowhere, going crazy, nothing happening, divorce, suicide, dropping out, or getting depressed are some of the Script finales that people have written for themselves.

Because they are a remnant of early development, Games are brought into an organization by organization members. Since Game players must find someone to play their Games with, the organization will be involved in Game playing more or less depending upon its selection of personnel. Game playing will be greater in an organization in which the management style includes a lot of Critical PARENT or Not-OK CHILD. Games can be interrupted or prevented by staying in the ADULT ego state or by allowing and encouraging CHILD to CHILD transactions.

In the next sections some typical Games played in organizations will be detailed.

Now I've Got You, You SOB

This is a competitive Game played from the position, "You can't trust people." The aim of the Game is to catch someone out in an untenable position or to manipulate him into a position in which he can be proved wrong. The payoff lies in the justification for rage, usually based on jealousy. The feeling of the Game-end comes through in the words, "Aha! Now I've got you!" The victim experiences a trapped, sinking feeling. The aggressor in this Game avoids confronting himself with his own deficiencies and has his existential position verified: "You can't trust people."

Both sides come away with negative strokes; however, in competitive situations in organizations, in addition the victim may lose face, have his idea defeated, be passed over for promotion, or in many ways become a scapegoat when the NIGYSOB is reinforced by others. NIGYSOBing in meetings is characterized by a persistent picking, criticizing, or maneuvering of a person into an untenable position. (See Figure 36.)

Someone who is being NIGYSOBed will usually be feeling the initial stages of the Game non-verbally, usually in the pit of his stomach. If he accepts the Game and begins to play, he will become defensive. The antithesis to this Game is to stay in the ADULT, refuse to take the hook to become defensive, and to stay with correct behavior. In working with NIGYSOBers it is very important to have a clear agreement on the rules of operation.

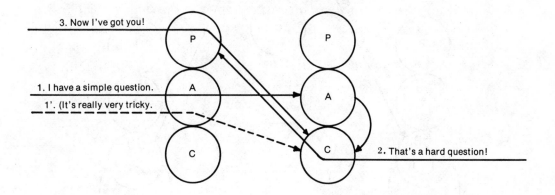

3. Now I've got you!

1. I have a simple question.

1'. (It's really very tricky.)

2. That's a hard question!

Figure 36. Schematic of "Now I've Got You, You SOB!"

Courtroom

As was described earlier, Courtroom is a rivalry Game having its origins in childhood in the family where the children did not feel that there were enough strokes to go around. Each Child had to compete for strokes and argue his case as to why he should receive the positive strokes while his sister or brother should receive none or at most negative strokes. The character roles in this Game are the plaintiff, defendant, judge and/or jury. The life position behind this Game is "I'm always wrong." The person aims to be reassured and says, "They've got to say I'm right." Typical examples of the situation leading into this Game are: quarreling children, a married couple seeking help, organizational staff or management members who are in conflict or competition appealing to their boss, usually separately, with stories of "He said" or "He did." (See Figure 37.)

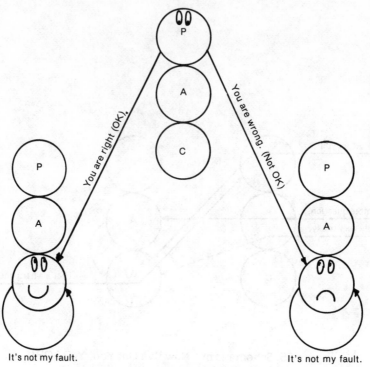

It's not my fault.   It's not my fault.

Figure 37. The Payoff in "Courtroom."

The advantages of this Game are excuse from guilt for oneself and projection of guilt onto someone else. That is, if I am convinced that I am always in the wrong, I will feel bad or guilty about the things that happen. If I can blame it all on someone else, this transfer of blame can make me feel good, at least superficially. The contestants in Courtroom get a lot of strokes from judge and jury, if there is one. The jury could, for example, be a committee.

The antithesis to this Game, unless the person to whom the appeal was taken enjoys being a judge, is to stay away from the PARENT and in the ADULT. He might say to each contestant in turn: "You're right. How do you feel about that?"

It is important to recognize that for someone whose life position is "I'm always wrong" or "I'm Not-OK" no amount of reassurance will satisfy him. Only when he decides that he **is OK** can he turn his energies to solving problems rather than proving he is right or wrong. It is also very helpful to prohibit talking about another person in the third person and insist that the arguers talk directly to each other, so that the feelings may be confronted directly. The discussion can then be turned from PARENT-CHILD and CHILD-CHILD to ADULT-ADULT problem solving based on the facts and the realities of the situation.

122

Look How Hard I've Tried

This is a failure-oriented Game which has at its base a feeling of helplessness from original injunctions of "Don't think" or "Don't take care of yourself." The person takes the position "I am helpless (or blameless)", and therefore, acts passively and with inner anger saying, "They can't push me around." The aim of the Game is vindication for the position. The person looks for freedom from guilt when he becomes aggressive and seeks to evade responsibility for his actions and decisions. In an organization this could be the person who comes into a new job sounding well-qualified and with good-sounding reasons for leaving several old jobs:

"That place is going downhill. No opportunity."

"They didn't appreciate my ideas."

"I tried my best, but everything went wrong."

"It's not my fault. I worked like a dog."

These statements could be accurate representations of reality or they could be cop-out statements denying responsibility for the events. Use of the word TRY is always a clue to an evasion of responsibility. Trying is what the CHILD says when it already knows that it won't succeed and so it is a "gamey" word. (See Figure 38.)

Some situations in which LHHIT may be heard:

In childhood: a child dressing,

In marriage: a spouse bucking for a divorce,

In an organization: a staff member bucking to get fired, demoted, or passed over for promotion.

Stroking, mostly negative, is obtained from the angry or belligerent exchanges that characterize the payoffs in this Game with the Game player becoming angry and defensive from his Adapted CHILD and deciding "What's the Use."

Case Illustration

A technician responsible for maintaining several small computers was doing excellent work and yet feeling angry and unappreciated. He was on call by a large number of computer users who

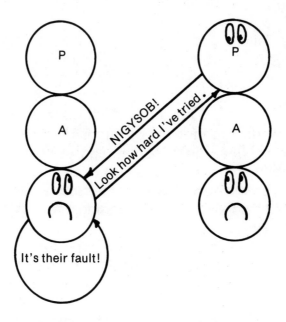

Figure 38. The Payoff in "Look How Hard I've Tried."

complained at their work being held up by "his" computer breaking down. The technician would work along without saying anything and suddenly blow up at one more complaint. His superior wanted to promote him but decided not to because of the poor relationship situation.

During a two-month series of TA training sessions, the technician learned about getting and giving negative and positive strokes, stamp collecting, and payoffs of negative strokes in Game playing. He decided to tell the complainers about his feelings and express his need for positive recognition. This broke up the Game "Look How Hard I'm Trying." He began to express anger appropriately and not to collect anger stamps, and to get more recognition and consideration from the computer users who felt a positive change in his attitude toward them. His supervisor commented on the positive changes in his behavior and recommended him for promotion.

This illustration demonstrates the statement that a Game requires two players so that when one player stops playing, the Game ends and the two sides can move into new stroking behavior.

Drunk and Proud of It

Alcoholism is frequently found among executive and management staff as well as in other sectors of life. Alcoholism has been analyzed into three main Games and is described in detail as a life style or Script by Claude Steiner in his book, **Games Alcoholics Play.**[1] The three kinds of Games are:

1. "Drunk and Proud" which will be discussed here because it is the one most likely to be seen in the organization;

2. "Lush" which is more of a home-drinking style and is most likely to appear in the wife of a busy executive;

3. "Wino" which is typified by the skid row wino and his circle. Usually the Wino is already out of the organization and is set on a path of self-destruction.

At the basis of Drunk and Proud is an injunction, "Don't express your feelings," or "Don't get angry." A child who is not allowed to get angry, no matter how provoked will look for other ways to express this feeling or will learn to set up situations in which no one can blame him for getting angry and/or aggressive. The aim of this Game is the guilt-free expression of anger and aggression. A good way to do this is to find someone who appears to be blameless and **very OK** and show up his weakness and Not-OKness by turning him into a Persecuter or Rescuer. In this way the player avoids blame for his anger.

So Drunk and Proud is played from a position of the very hard working person who takes on more than he can be reasonably expected to accomplish. He says, "Everybody tries to tell me what to do." He implies, "I'm bad; you're good (Hah!)." He then proceeds to prove that you are "Not-OK" by getting you to either persecute him or to forgive him. The roles in this three-handed Game are the Alcoholic, the Persecuter, and the Rescuer. One person, wife or boss, can play roles of Persecuter and Rescuer at different times.

The usual Persecuter or Rescuer for this type of Alcoholic

is his wife who will either scold him or forgive him—in either case he is getting strokes for his misbehavior and validating his "You're OK (Ha, Ha)" position.

This Game also allows for a lot of time-structuring associated with drinking Pastimes, such as Martini, Morning After and Shot and Pills. He also gets a lot of strokes from his drinking companions, especially after a hard day of business when he received very few strokes—and when he did not allow himself to get angry for working too hard or being expected to do too much.

The Game is seen in childhood in the form of "Try and Stop Me," messing with food, telling obvious lies, and getting parents angry over trivia. In later life it appears in excessive and uncontrolled drinking with subsequent problems. Examples can be seen throughout the corporate structure. (See Figure 39.)

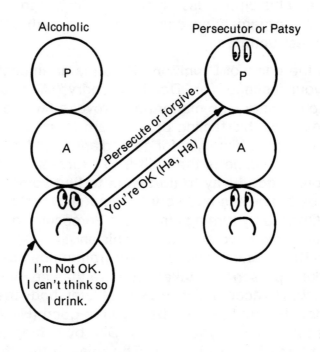

Figure 39. Alcoholism; Drunk and Proud type.

126

Choice and Antithesis in Game Playing

Games can be mildly, moderately, or severely destructive depending upon the strength and destructiveness of the injunction behind them and the degree of intensity with which they are played. The Game player is attempting to make sense out of living and is responding in the only way that he was able to figure life out when he was young. It should be understood that his goal is to make himself comfortable; his goal is **not** to make others uncomfortable. Since it takes at least two players to play a Game, the player must find others who will play his Game and accept his ulterior invitation to play for their own reasons. His Games complement theirs so that both sides get the strokes that they need and want. Games in organizations, as elsewhere, can be detected by the repetitive manner with which they occur. They can be stopped by a decision on the part of either player to stop the Game. As people make the decision to play a Game initially, they can also make a new decision to get strokes in another way. Behind modern management training approaches such as sensitivity training and other methods of feedback or confrontation is the idea of stopping indirect and ulterior transactions, and encouraging persons to ask for what they want in a straight way. The intention is to develop human relationships with positive feelings or strokes, so that people will stop setting up transactions in order to get negative strokes. (See Figure 40.)

The consultant works to break up the Games and to get people to talk straight about what is really bothering them, so that the problems have a chance of being solved instead of being perpetuated.

Hard Games, such as Alcoholic, can be given up through TA counseling and psychotherapy, through which the person gets permission to stop drinking, examine his Script and injunctions, disobey the early injunctions or "Don't," rewrite his Script into a livable, positive stroke-getting style, and decide to get on with life within his own unique capacity!

127

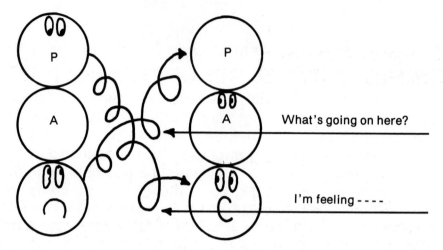

Figure 40. Stopping Games / It takes two to play.

Application and Exercises

1. In what situations do you find yourself getting negative strokes?
2. What kind of people do you get most negative strokes from?
3. What kinds of negative strokes do you see others giving in your organization?
4. Check back in Chapter One for the conditions that define a Game in the TA sense. What Games are played in your organization? How do they start?
   a) What is the ulterior invitation?
   b) The switch of ego states?
   c) The payoff?
5. What Games were played in your family?
6. What is your part in any Games that you are involved in? What does the Game accomplish for you?
7. If you stopped playing these Games what could happen?
8. What Games do you want to stop?
9. What will you do instead?

REFERENCE

1. Steiner, C. **Games Alcoholics Play.** Grove Press, New York, 1971.

Chapter Seven:
CRISIS: CAUSES, EFFECTS, TREATMENT

What Is Crisis?

Crisis is the moment of collision, the moment when change must occur. It results from a build up of forces or circumstances to the point where the need or demand for change becomes unavoidable. As the world is a dynamic system, change of course occurs all of the time but usually at a rate that is not very noticeable. In a time of crisis events are speeded up and decisions must be made quickly while attempting to avoid as many unpleasant and undesirable consequences as possible.

A moment of crisis may last an infinitesimal fraction of a second (as in the case of collision of atomic particles), a second or so (as in the collision of two cars), hours, days, weeks, or months (as in the case of collisions between people or organizations), years (as in the case of conflicts between nations), or eons (as in the case of colliding galaxies in outer space). The distinguishing feature of crisis is that the outcome is not known. Something happens to a system and choices are available. The patient may get well or he may die. The organization may turn around or it may go on to bankruptcy. The couple may become reconciled or get divorced. The person may decide to commit suicide or to stay alive. The people in the cars may get injured or not, more or less seriously, or they may walk away from the wrecks. The play may be accepted, rejected, or modified. Decisions must be made, perhaps by the human mind if there is time for choice, perhaps by the laws of nature which also allow choices on a statistical basis.

Crisis can be brought on by an illness, by a hurricane, by war, by peace, by disagreement of values between people, by death or illness of an executive, by danger to life, by danger to profits, by danger to love, by the cancellation of an order, by change of a budget, by a change of plans, by a machine breaking down, by disaster, or by boredom.

For individuals, crisis is brought on by a threat to the essentials of his life: food, shelter, or strokes. For organizations, crisis is brought on by a threat to the structure or continued existence of the organization. These threats may occur as a result of the natural forces of nature, as with earthquake, tornadoes, storms, flood, drought, or pestilence. They may also occur as a result of the interactions between men and women who have different wants and needs, or who want or need the same things—which are in short supply.

When an individual faces a crisis not caused by forces of nature, "acts of God," or truly accidental events, it may be a deliberate (whether in or out of awareness) part of a life plan or Script which calls for the development of crisis as is typically found in drama, which is a reflection of real life. In a play the story builds up toward the crisis at which point some drastic events take place leading to a resolution, often to a surprising switch, sometimes felt to be inevitable. In real life drama, the child, having made his early decisions as to the course and outcome of his life, will live in such a way as to move inexorably toward a crisis by which the expected Script outcome—suicide, divorce, death by alcohol or drugs, giving up, nothing happening until death, running away, going crazy, or any other—ends the story. Even though the individual is aware of the outcome, he moves steadily toward it. This "trapped" movement is the tragedy of the Script-bound hero or heroine—the inexorability of "fate."

A similar situation may take place in an organization. At some stage in its growth a life style may be settled on which carries with it the seeds of destruction and bankruptcy. Even though many voices warn of the problems ahead, the warnings are ignored or discounted, resulting in lack of planning, inadequate fiscal control, inadequate reserves, little or no investment in research and development, lack of management development and depth, and so on. The organization moves toward and into crisis and suddenly choices have to be made. Changes must occur. The outcome is in doubt. Confusion sets in. Scapegoats are sought. Committees are quickly formed. Consultants are called in. Transfusions of money are made. Negative stroking increases and morale drops.

Effects of Crisis

IN AN OK POSITION—ORGANIZATIONS

The approach of a crisis in the life of a well-functioning individual stimulates the organization of defenses. The adrenal glands prepare the body for a quick reaction. The ADULT begins gathering facts about the situation and begins to calculate the probabilities for escape, rescue, or recovery by the paths available. Communication with others is increased in order to have a maximum of information available for decision making. The CHILD is allowed to feel all of the feelings of fear, anger, hurt, and pain that it experiences and gets all the nurturing that the Nurturing PARENT has at its disposal. CHILD and PARENT are in close contact with each other while the ADULT goes about the business of getting on with handling the crisis in the best possible way. Old fears which are brought to the surface in times of stress are recognized as old fears, experienced, and put aside. (See Figure 41.)

IN AN OK POSITION — ORGANIZATIONS

Similar events occur in the well-functioning organization. When a crisis situation is seen approaching or occurs, the immediate communication of the facts to all parts of the organization alerts the members to the situation. Management meets on appropriate levels and begins the job of sorting out the data and begins to make alternate plans to meet the crisis. All available resources of leadership and funds are checked and made ready. As fear, panic, or anger spread throughout the organization, the management is ready with constant communication of the facts and plans of action. It also recognizes the fears, acknowledges the dangers, and expresses its concern and determination to live through the crisis and to support its members as well as it can. At this point the trust level which the management has built up in the past is a crucial factor in the allaying of fear. This trust of

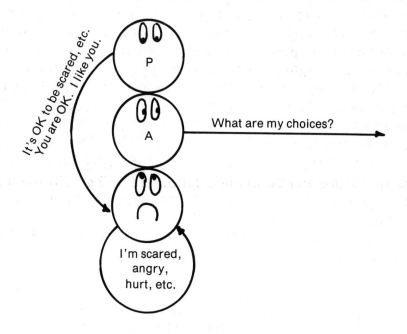

Figure **41**. Crisis from an OK position.

management is similar to the need for the CHILD to trust the
PARENT for support.

IN A NOT-OK POSITION — INDIVIDUALS

When an individual has selected a life plan or Script for
himself that includes a position of "I'm Not-OK" or "You're Not-
OK," then the effects of crisis are different. If the person has been
living in his Counterscript in order to ward off the painful implica-
tions of Script messages of failure, lack of positive strokes and
fulfilling human relationships, then crisis always will increase
the likelihood of switching from the Counterscript, which may be
a "work hard, be successful" position, to a depressed or perse-
cuted position dictated by the Script. The crisis can be one occurring from causes completely separate from the person's intent,
or the crisis can be set up by the person in order to bring about
the crisis that his Script calls for.

132

For example, a person who has a failure Script may have the misfortune to live during an economic depression and lose his job for that reason. In good times, however, he will have to find some way to fail anyway, so he will go about setting up the situation for failure. He may do this by taking on a job that is too difficult or too demanding, or by selecting people to work with who will play his failure Game. They are expected to be dissatisfied with him or overly critical so that he can eventually say, "See, I knew that I couldn't make it. What do you expect of a guy with a wooden leg (or some other excuse)?"

If the Script is reflected in a "They're Not-OK" position, then the failure will be blamed on others: "They did me in," or "You see. You can't trust anybody. They're all out to screw you." (See Figure 42.)

Thus, the Not-OK position exaggerates the effect of crisis and stands in the way of adequate problem-solving.

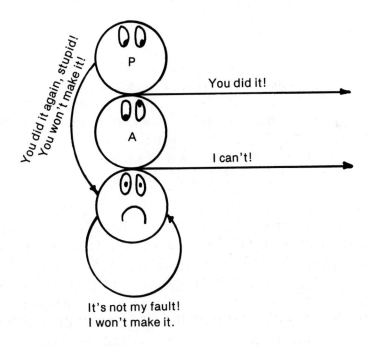

Figure 42. *Crises from a Not-OK position*

IN A NOT-OK POSITION — ORGANIZATIONS

In organizations both of these approaches can be taken when a poorly functioning organization approaches or is in a crisis. As the effects of crisis are on the CHILD level of fear of hurt or deprivation or loss of stroking, so in an organization the crisis is felt on its emotional level as a threat, usually from the external environment, to the continuation of the organization as it presently exists. Equilibrium is upset and the natural reaction is to restore the equilibrium. This effect also occurs in families and is known as homeostasis, the tendency to restore equilibrium.

If the organization does not have a well-functioning management system on the ADULT level, or if management's ADULT is contaminated with CHILD fantasy or illusion, or with PARENT prejudice and tradition, then the response to crisis may seem crazy, just as some individual's response to the external world seems crazy to others. The cardinal rule is that organizations and individuals will do what they can do to make themselves comfortable. If decision-making is contaminated, then the results may have an unreal aspect which is called "crazy."

If management operates with some hidden rules about not trusting people, then in a time of crisis this may result in a closing down of communication—and at a time when communication becomes most important. If the management position is heavily in the "I'm OK, They're Not-OK" position, then at a time of crisis much time may be spent in hunting for a scapegoat or scapegoats on whom to hang the blame, instead of getting on with the job of change and problem solving.

If the management position is one of weakness in a cruel world, the "We're Not-OK, They're Not-OK" position, then the reaction to crisis may be one of withdrawal behind a defense line with the intent of holding off change as long as possible, or of a throwing up of hands and asking someone else to take over and solve the problems. The possible ways of reacting to crisis as a reflection of the basic life position of management can be nicely illustrated by the "OK Corral" devised by Franklin Ernst.[1] This is shown in Figure 43. In the face of crisis individuals or organizations will take a primary stance in one of these four areas.

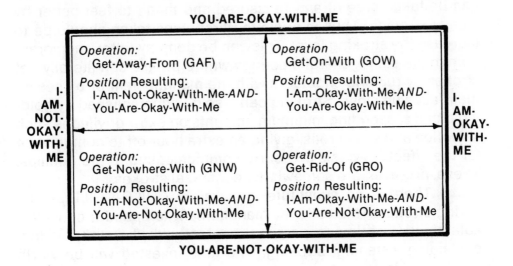

YOU-ARE-OKAY-WITH-ME

Operation:
   Get-Away-From (GAF)
 	
Position Resulting:
   I-Am-Not-Okay-With-Me-*AND-*
   You-Are-Okay-With-Me
	Operation
	   Get-On-With (GOW)
	
	Position Resulting:
	   I-Am-Okay-With-Me-*AND-*
	   You-Are-Okay-With-Me

Operation:
   Get-Nowhere-With (GNW)
 	
Position Resulting:
   I-Am-Not-Okay-With-Me-*AND-*
   You-Are-Not-Okay-With-Me
	Operation:
	   Get-Rid-Of (GRO)
	
	Position Resulting:
	   I-Am-Okay-With-Me-*AND-*
	   You-Are-Not-Okay-With-Me

I-AM-NOT-OKAY-WITH-ME (left) **I-AM-OKAY-WITH-ME** (right)

YOU-ARE-NOT-OKAY-WITH-ME

Figure 43.   The OK Corral: Grid for GET-ON-WITH

The results of any position except the Get-On-With position of ADULT computing will be reflected in confusion, drop of morale, loss of communication within the organization, fighting or fleeing the problems, and a pervasive atmosphere of fear, anger, and loss of positive stroking.

Treatment of Crisis

The most crucial step that anyone or any organization can take in crisis is to turn on his or its ADULT. Feelings of fear, anger, hurt are real and are best expressed and not discounted. These are in the CHILD and cannot be avoided. Sharing of these feelings and acceptance of human reactions builds trust on a fundamental level so that the CHILD will let the ADULT get on with its decision-making computations with a minimum of interference. It's hard enough to collect data and make decisions under pressure of time without having to control an overabundance of inner turmoil.

135

As the CHILD, either individual or collective, has little sense of the future or the past but wants strokes here and now, it can be taken care of and reassured and made to feel better by steady stroking. Thus in crisis the first steps taken should be to increase the stroking level. This can be done by letter, memorandum to the staff, general meetings where people can literally get strokes by rubbing shoulders with the management or by seeing their faces up close. Stroking can also be accomplished by holding picnics, spending minimum amounts on extra privileges such as coffee and sweet rolls, giving an extra hour off to compensate for the effects of crisis pressure, communicating to the families. These, however, are somewhat mechanical strokes.

There is no substitute for straight CHILD-CHILD warm, caring strokes. This calls for management to spend a considerable amount of time in personal contact with the staff, talking, explaining, listening, stroking. The time invested will be worth the cost in improved morale, motivation, and creativity. Human resource is the most valuable commodity in an organization and positive stroking activates this resource. There are an unlimited number of ways to increase stroking. Strokes do not cost anything and, contrary to the popular notion, strokes are not limited in supply—like gold. Thus they need not obey the usual laws of supply and demand. (See Figure 44.)

In times of pressure and fear the CHILD may withdraw and the person turn on his Critical and Domineering PARENT. The PARENT will handle the crisis based on experience of others in the past. This may or may not be useful at the present time. (See Figure 45.) This reaching for a parent figure to get us out of trouble appears in nations where in times of trouble the people turn to strong figures, military or civilian, to tell them what to do. Likewise an organization may turn to an autocratic chairman or president to manage the affairs of the company. In this way the staff avoids the necessity of working together and sharing the responsibility of decision making.

Turning on the ADULT in an organization means turning on the attitude of responsibility of the management and staff toward solving their own problems and making difficult and painful decisions when necessary. It means taking care of business instead of finding a scapegoat. It means getting on with life and

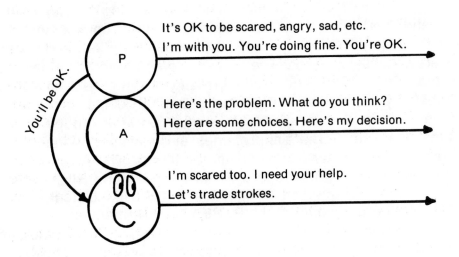

Figure 44. *An OK manager working with crisis*

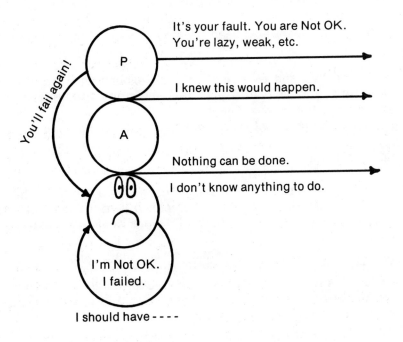

Figure 45. *A Not-OK manager working with crisis*

work instead of living in the past or becoming helpless with anxiety about the future. It means improving communication, clarifying information, getting help, food, supplies, and funds where necessary. It means setting up protection for the members of the organization. The rational, reality testing, data handling, probability computing ADULT management begins to organize its leadership and resources, to set up working groups to lay plans, examine alternate approaches, and consider changes that are made necessary by the crisis conditions. The ADULT management listens to the needs and wants of the staff CHILD, listens to the helpful, supportive advice, or the critical, insistent, prejudiced, autocratic voice of the PARENT of the management, and makes decisions based on the realities in such a way as to aim for the safety and security of the organization and its members.

Case Illustration

A new company was heading into crisis from lack of capital because a new product line was slow in establishing a market. Feelings of discouragement, frustration, fear, and anger were increasing. The chief executive and chief investor was experiencing considerable conflict between his ADULT judgment about cutting losses and finding ways to bring in new financing, and CHILD/PARENT feelings of guilt and responsibility toward the staff, including marginal members.

Midway through a several-month series of TA training he decided to clarify his contracts with the executive members of the company.

He had an interview with each executive and sent a summary of their positions and contract for the coming year to each person for feedback so that each party would have a clear understanding of mutual expectations.

In the course of this negotiation several marginal or sub-marginal staff members left the organization. As the crisis period unfolds, the executive is feeling more comfortable about going ahead with various ADULT-programmed alternatives.

When the CHILD is reassured and the ADULT has begun to operate, then the crisis is over and the future has begun.

Application and Exercises

1. What are the crises in your life now? In your organiza-
   zation?
2. What does your PARENT say about these crises? Your
   ADULT? Your CHILD?
3. What are the stroking levels and the ratio of positive to
   negative strokes occurring in each crisis situation?
4. In these crises, which people take an I'm OK, You're
   OK position?
   — I'm Not-OK, You're OK position?
   — I'm OK, You're Not-OK position?
   — I'm Not-OK, You're Not-OK position?
   Classify the people according to the OK Corral in
   Figure 43.
5. Let your mind go in fantasy for each of these crises.
   What are the worst things that could happen? Follow
   the line of worst things to the end so as to hear your
   CHILD's fears and worst expectations.
6. Turn on your ADULT and check on the amount of reality in each of these fears.
7. In time of crisis which of your ego states comes on
   strongest? Which next? How do you finally resolve the
   crisis?
8. How does your organization react to crisis? What is
   the predominant ego state that first comes on? Which
   next? Who are the most effective people in a crisis?
   What ego state do you see them operating out of?
9. Which people in your organization react least effectively to crisis? What ego states do you perceive them
   using? What kinds of ways do they have for handling
   crisis?
10. What happens to stroking levels and stroke ratios in
    your organization in times of crisis? To communica-
    tion in general? Which managers give more positive
    strokes? Which ones withdraw? Which look for a
    scapegoat to negative stroke?

11. What do you want to change in your behavior as a manager in time of crisis? How will you go about it? When will you start?

REFERENCE

1. Ernst, F., Jr. "The OK Corral: The Grid for Get On With," **Transactional Analysis Journal,** 1:4, p. 231 (1971).

Chapter Eight:
CHANGE, RENEWAL, AND GROWTH

Signs of Needs

There are a number of indicators to watch for in an organization which indicate that growth, change, and renewal are crucial tasks.

► *CRISIS.* As is clear from the last section, crisis is a call for help or a signal bell. Something must be done or changed if the individual or organization is not to go under. Crisis is the clearest sign that growth, change, and/or renewal is needed.

► *STAGNATION, BOREDOM, WITHDRAWAL.* An organization is facing trouble when the management or staff begin to feel or to complain of stagnation or boredom and signs of withdrawal are seen. This is an indication that the CHILD is not getting the strokes that it needs to keep its spine from shriveling. Nothing is happening. Excitement is lacking. People are going their own way and withdrawing from involvement with the organization. There is nothing in it (no strokes) for them. This results in a decrease in the joy of work and the excitement of seeing something completed. There is not much pleasure in work and the staff or management are getting little satisfaction from seeing the organization grow and change.

► *DEPRESSION, DISSATISFACTION.* Another indication of need is when the managers begin to show signs of depression. As stress increases, drinking also increases. The atmosphere in the offices and plant begins to get quiet and restrained: Hallways are quiet. Grievances and complaints begin to increase. Problems which were once easily solved now take many long meetings at which the discussions go round and round, and there is no strong desire to solve the problems. Long-range planning becomes uninteresting. Nobody cares about tomorrow; they do not expect to be there and have no interest in planning for others to follow.

▶ *ANGER AND CONFLICT.* Conflict is another sign of need. Most anger is a substitute for the feelings of hurt, fear, or deprivation. Conflict over an auxiliary subject is a common way to avoid talking about the real feelings, when this is felt to be too risky. Thus the appearance of conflict between management or staff members where none existed before, is a sign that renewed growth and examination of changes is needed in order to provide the stroking that people desire.

Conflict will appear in two forms. It can be CHILD-CHILD between people who want the same thing and are fighting for it as a result of the economy, or it can appear as PARENT-CHILD putting down of the other in order to use PARENTal authority and power to avoid expressing the CHILD fears, hurts, or wants. (See Figure 46.)

▶ *AGING AND BUREAUCRATIZATION.* What is commonly referred to as "aging" of staff or management may only be a loss of creativity and excitement due to boredom, lack of adequate stroking, or lack of stimulation. When the Creative CHILD or "Little Professor" withdraws, then the personality loses its glow, its verve and dash, and its spontaneity. Bureaucratization of an organization is another symptom of this process. There is a great deal of safety in fixed procedures and rituals. The stroking level may not be very high but the risks are minimized, so when a management does not show concern for stroking levels, this seems like

142

Figure 46.   Anger and conflict

a good way for the CHILD to hold on to his gains. This is connected to the problem of mid-life demotivation of managers and staff, and is discussed in detail in the next chapter "Middle-escence and Management."

▶ *LACK OF CREATIVITY.* Along with withdrawal by the CHILD's "Little Professor" goes a loss in creativity and the new ideas that come with it. This is a great loss to an organization as few can live for long in a changing world without the input of new ideas. When children are young, they are very creative, as they must figure out how to live in their families and how to get their needs filled. Although they have little information on how the world operates, they come up with very creative solutions using their intuitions and all their senses. During the growing up and civilizing process, (which largely consists of imposing PARENTal programing on the CHILD), the creative spirit is gradu-

143

ally suppressed in favor of adaptive behavior where the results are more certain.

Some families encourage creative behavior; their children grow up to be the leaders and winners in management as well as in other parts of life. Some kids decide to be winners in spite of family pressures. Creative behavior needs stroking in order for it to be continually reinforced. This is especially important as one grows older and more experienced in the rewards of work and living, and is then less driven by cultural requirements of home and family-building.

Stroking needs are internal, from one's own PARENT to CHILD, and external, generally from other people's PARENT and CHILD to one's own CHILD. Thus, keeping creative people creative means supplementing the strokes that they give themselves with stroking from the management and from their peers.

► *PASTIMES, GAMES, RACKETS.* When the above described signs of need for change, renewal, and growth are present, they are accompanied by the transactional processes involving Pastimes, Games, and Rackets. In Pastiming, the meetings seldom get down to the real problems. Discussing the agenda order or some current but non-significant problem, can serve to avoid meeting the actual crisis head on and getting on with the search for best solutions and choices. Game-playing will also be present at all levels of management in places of decision making. Game-playing provides the players with the negative stroking that they live on where positive stroking is not available and advances their Scripts independently of what is going on with the organization. The staff will be presenting the kinds of emotional responses that they were trained to give in their early families. These are their Rackets.

Rackets are a way of behaving or expressing feelings by indirect artificial or phony sounding means so as to obtain recognition or stroking from others. They are used, for example, when a person feels afraid to ask directly for what he or she wants or to express true feelings openly. Rackets usually reflect behavior and emotional responses learned in early family life. In an emergency, one person may cover up fear with anger, another may cover fear with withdrawal, another may cover fear with sadness and depression, or with a smiling or grinning face. Rackets differ from Games in that there is no sudden switch of ego states. If a switch does occur in the course of Racketing transactions, then a Game ensues and moves on to the final Game payoff.

EFFECT ON PRODUCTION, PRODUCTIVITY, GROWTH

All of the above mentioned processes will result in a drop in production, productivity, profitability, and an increased toll in human discomfort. The use of ego-grams to detect special needs for change and renewal can lead the way to renewed growth. Figure 47 shows the ego-gram expected for staff in an organization in or approaching crisis.

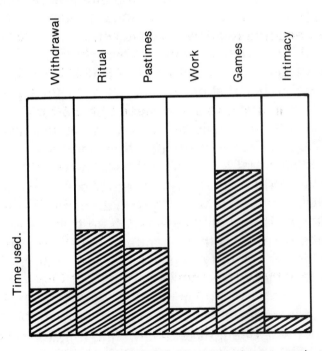

Figure 47. *The need for growth, change, and renewal shows up in the time structure diagram*

Necessary Conditions for Growth, Change, Renewal

► *AWARENESS AND DECISION.* The most important condition for change is a decision that the present situation is too painful or too destructive to allow to continue and therefore change must occur. This is a very difficult decision for an individual to make as it acknowledges that the way he has been leading his life and making decisions is no longer suitable or effective. Change means risk and fear of the unknown.

The same process holds true for an organization. The decision to change may depend on a group of managers and this joint decision is crucial. However, the recognition of the presence of a problem or an oncoming crisis and the recognition of the pain and discomfort in an organization are an admission of weakness, mistakes, or failure, so people usually put up very strong defenses against such an admission.

The signs of need for change, renewal, and growth have been detailed in the preceding section. The management must allow itself to examine the facts critically (in the ADULT reality testing sense) without becoming critical of itself or its staff (in the PARENT-CHILD put-down sense). This distinction between Critical PARENT and Critical ADULT is essential to decision making. Creative (CHILD) thinking is quickly extinguished in the face of Critical PARENT. If on the other hand a sense of participation in reality testing is present, the CHILD will feel excited rather than squelched and will support Critical ADULT reality testing. The management must also communicate the reality to the staff so that they will also become convinced that change is necessary and that their needs for security and strokes are well recognized by management.

Both management and staff must decide that change, renewal, and growth are needed. They must also want these changes and be willing to take the risks inherent with change. Wants and needs relate to CHILD feelings and tap into the power of the CHILD, which in the

146

end is most important. Unless a person wants to change, he will not—except under extreme and continual duress. Unless the members of an organization want to change, the various types of resistance will continually crop up in the change process to gum up the work, causing interference with the process or stopping it altogether.

It's always hard to understand why change is so difficult for the other person. The path is obvious. Why do people keep looking for failure and negative strokes when there is so much good advice around as to how they can change for their own good? The answer to this seeming paradox lies again in the fantasy life of the CHILD in each person. The CHILD is very practical and does not want to give up anything, neither positive nor negative strokes. CHILD knows what it's got and will give up something only if it trusts and is convinced that it will get something better in return. We have been trained to be and to think certain ways by our parents and our culture, and changing means doing something against the ways that we were taught. This means changing the value system, the PARENT, and is a frightening prospect. (See Figure 48.)

Thus, a first question that a management might ask of someone who proposes change is "How do you know that it will work and be better?" At least this is a question put by a PARENTally operating management. An ADULT management might respond: "Let's see the facts, evaluate the risks, and make a decision."

► *THE COUNSELOR OR CONSULTANT.* Because of the tendency of any organization, family, or individual to rationalize its irrationalities in order to support the status quo, an important addition is that of the consultant, change agent, or counselor. This (or these) person(s) are trained to be aware of unexpressed feelings, of the presence of Games, Pastimes, Rackets, or other methods of avoiding change. A well-managed organization will have some of its own staff trained in the behavioral science techniques necessary to facilitate change. (See Figure 49.)

147

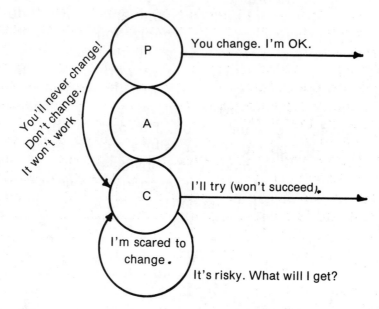

Figure 48.   The difficulty of change

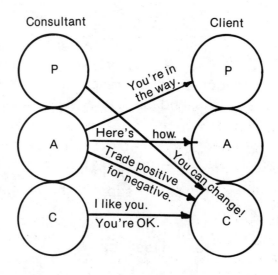

Figure 49.   The Counselor-Consultee transactions

The field of organizational development has grown in recent years as the means for organizational change. Consultants are selected by recommendation and by exploring the possibility of trust between the management and the consultants. They can be an invaluable aid to change in organizations even as a competent counselor or psychotherapist can be a great aid to individual change. The literature on change in human beings is voluminous and often vague. Basically, change involves the resolution of conflict between the wants and needs of the CHILD and the demands and controls of the PARENT. These conflicts interfere with the ability of the ADULT of the consultant to mediate between CHILD and PARENT and to get for the person what he wants.

Change in individuals can sometimes begin quickly even as the healing process begins when one removes a splinter; however, the changes extend over months and years. (See Figure 50.) In organizations which consist of large numbers of individuals, change and growth is a matter of years; thus, an adequate consultation contract recognizes this fact so that a flashy beginning is not mistaken for the end result. Not until the organization has obtained a new autonomy and the ability to analyze and act on its own emotional problems, is the work of the consultant completed.

► *PROGRAMING AND PLANNING FOR CHANGE.* In recognition of of these realities, a necessary condition for a successful project for change in an organization is the allotment of adequate funds, time, and place for the necessary education, and training and counseling to take place. The processes of change are different from the usual daily problem-solving as they involve emotional contact that is not in the usual executive routine. It is easy for people to get scared by their own emotional intensity, and adequate support and protection are needed for those in the process of change. The allotment of time for the processes of management is essential, and so is the allotment of time

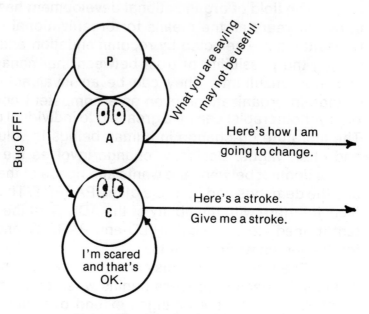

Figure 50.   The beginning of change

for planning and change, together with the insecurities and anxieties coming with change. Commitment by the primary management is of critical importance.

Contracting for Change

The contract for organizational change is the first step. People know what they want and will say what they want if they dare. Thus, a contract of this type can only be made under conditions of trust. A contract is made between ADULTs but if the CHILD does not approve, it is then a wasted document. The needs and wants of the stockholders, board of directors, management at various levels, and staff are the same in terms of the basic human need for strokes, but there are different strokes for different folks and each group must decide for itself what it wants. The contract for change must recognize what each group wants. If the contract ends up looking very idealistic, that is OK as a start.

The process of turning a contract into reality will involve rewriting and revising the contract. The parties will get new and different views of what they want as the process continues. A counseling contract has the same requirements as a legal contract. There must be:

1. Mutual consent: between ADULT ego states and also CHILD ego states.
2. Valid consideration: the benefits conferred by the consultant and the benefits conferred by the organization (fees).
3. Competency: the contract must be between legally liable and mentally competent people.
4. Legal object: the contract must not be in violation of the law.

Application and Exercises

1. Look for departments and managers or personnel showing signs of stagnation, boredom, or withdrawal. What signs are there that stroking levels are low? Check with the people concerned to verify your guesses or observations.
2. Turn on your intuitive Little Professor and wander around your organization, stopping here and there to listen, say a few sentences to some people and generally sense the atmosphere. When you are back in your office, write down a quick list of your intuitive impressions without any PARENTal censoring or comments.
3. After each meeting or conference that you attend for one week, write down the visible or subsurface signs of anger and conflict. Which people are in conflict? What do you guess is the source of their anger? Is the anger expressed openly or do the organization rules require indirect means of expressing hostility? What Games are being played instead of open expression of feelings? Are problem-solving and long-range planning proceeding smoothly, erratically, or not at all?

151

4. Make a list of the managers or personnel that you consider "aging" in the sense of a strongly decreased contribution to the organization. Compare the people now with their contributions ten years or twenty years ago. What has changed?

   If possible, check with these people as to their ideas on what has changed and what is important for them now as compared with ten or twenty years ago.

   What changes can be made to re-interest or re-excite their CHILD?

5. How do you get your ideas? Under what conditions do you feel most creative? If you wanted to double your creativity, what would you do?

6. What are the predominant Pastimes, Games, and Rackets going on in your organization?

7. Make a drawing of your estimate of the changes in productivity, production, and growth in your organization for the past several years. How does this compare with your expectation? What do your PARENT, ADULT, and CHILD say about this comparison?

8. In your organization who makes decisions about change? How are these decisions made? By what ego state? How are the decisions communicated to the other managers and staff?

9. What changes would you make in your organization, speaking from each of your ego states?

10. Write out contracts for change that you would like to make with each of the five people with whom you associate closely.

11. Keeping in mind that change will be resisted by CHILD unless he sees something in it for him, how would you go about making these changes under conditions of increased positive stroking?

12. During the change process, who will be accepted as potent leaders of change? How will permission for change be given? How will protection be offered?

13. Where do you see impasses developing toward change in your organization? What do you think are the CHILD feelings behind the impasse?

14. What personal contracts for change do you want to make? Write out the contracts and include:
    a) a time scale for the proposed change,
    b) what resources you will need for the change,
    c) what difficulties will have to be overcome,
    d) what feelings you expect during the change process,
    e) some details of how you will proceed and when you will begin the change.

Chapter Nine:
MIDDLE-ESCENCE AND MANAGEMENT

The Middle Management Blues

One of the persistent, painful, and pervasive phenomena of organizational life is the steady increase, at the middle management levels of a growing organization, of managers who were once highly considered for their contributions to the organization's program, and who lately have become a problem. As the middle management level comprises a large fraction of managerial talent and cost, the "problem" manager cannot be long ignored in hopes that his problem will go away.

What appears on the surface is a decrease of motivation, a lowering of interest and commitment to organizational problem solving and goal setting, reduced "productivity" in the sense of contributions towards reaching organizational goals, whether they be level, increasing or decreasing profits, or services to their customers or clients.

These managers are often carelessly referred to as "deadwood" and challenge organizational leadership to find a satisfactory compromise in the variables of effectiveness and caring. These men and women were once the most effective and potent young people in the organization. What has happened to them? What can or should be done about them?

The Script Issue

Each individual's Script calls for him to be either a Winner, a Non-winner or a Loser.[1] Winners will become the president of the company or will not, and will feel like a winner, gets lots of strokes, have fun, and be effective at work in any position in the organization. Losers are not likely to reach the middle management level in an organization run on a merit system, so Loser Scripts will not be discussed.

Non-winners can be divided into two categories, Almost-Winners and Almost-Losers. The Almost-Winner follows the Sisyphus Script, trying over and over to roll the ball up the hill, only to have it roll back down just as she was about to make it. The Almost-Loser walks along the edge of the precipice and almost falls over periodically and just manages to pull himself back from the edge in time. Some statements characterizing these Script positions are given in Table 5.

The managers to be considered here fall usually in the Almost-Winner class with an Achiever type of Script structure. Some Almost-Losers will also appear; for example, the manager who has been quite effective even though his heavy drinking has almost gotten him fired.

The Almost-Winners were highly motivated in their early years in school and in the company, were hard driving and hard driven by their Script injunctions. At some time in their lives, (usually in the forties) something happens, and another kind of behavior begins to appear that looks like a Loser Script. This could be diagnosed as an "After" Script, "You can enjoy yourself for a while, but after that your troubles begin." Another possibility is that the original life plan runs out after a certain age. Then the problem becomes what to do next. The way in which Achiever Scripts run out can be called "the Red Hot Poker Effect."

An Achiever Script is based on conditional stroking. The child gets strokes for what he does rather than for what he is. Jill gets stroked for reading at age three and for her top grades in school, but not for expressing her feelings, asking for hugs, and being a fun-loving little girl. Jack gets strokes for hitting a home run on the school playground, for building a super construction with his Erector Set, and when the teacher says that he is the best in the class, and not for expressing his feelings, playing house, being the daddy taking care of the babies, and crying when he is hurt.

WINNERS

I am OK, responsible, committed. I approve of myself.

I can win (succeed).

I am strong, smart, etc.

It's OK to get scared, angry, sad, etc.

It's OK to have fun.

It's OK to give strokes and ask for strokes.

I can run my own life.

I can depend on others.

I can risk being close to others.

ALMOST WINNERS

I am usually OK and usually approve of myself.

I can almost win (succeed).

Don't be better than —.

Be cautious about feelings.

Work first. Fun later (maybe).

Give and get some strokes, but not too many.

Run your own life with the following limits: —.

Be cautious about others.

ALMOST LOSERS

I am not really OK; don't really approve of myself.

I won't actually lose (fail).

Express only certain feelings (not anger for example).

Fun is not important.

Give and get mostly negative strokes.

Listen to others and usually do what they say.

Watch out for others.

LOSERS

I am Not OK.

I expect to lose.

I am weak, dumb, etc.

It's Not OK to have fun.

It's Not OK to give strokes and to ask for strokes.

I can't run my own life.

I can't depend on others.

Table 5. Winners, Almost-Winners, Almost-Losers, and Losers

Jack and Jill get plenty of strokes from their folks, but they get the idea that achievement is where it's at rather than in relationships. Script injunctions and Counterscript drivers are taken in and fashioned by the Little Professor into Red Hot Pokers of internal drivers, which they use as they grow up to keep themselves motivated and internally stroked as they move toward "success" in life. While they feel reasonably OK about themselves, they have been trained to be motivated primarily by internal stroking for achievement and not to expect external stroking in large quantities, but only a few now and then at the end of some successful project.

Table 6 shows a list of some typical Red Hot Pokers.

The Red Hot Poker Effect

SCRIPT INJUNCTIONS	COUNTERSCRIPT DRIVERS[4]
Don't have fun!	Work hard!
Don't be satisfied!	Work harder! Try harder!
Don't be who you are!	Be famous! Be best!
Parents' needs come first!	Serve others! Be pleasing!
Don't ask for yourself!	Help others Rescue!
Don't express feelings!	Be strong!
Don't be free!	Hurry up! Be pleasing!

Table 6: Red Hot Pokers

An important answer to the question, "What makes Sammy—or Sandy—run?" is "Red Hot Pokers." The Script trail is likely to lead through high grades in school, valedictorian rank, high athletic achievement, making the teams, top positions in extracurricular activities in high school and college, ratings of "Most likely to succeed" in the yearbook, without a corresponding success in making close friends and loving relationships. Sammy and Sandy are often seen by others or feel themselves to be loners.

Episcripts[3] and Antiscripts[4] can also lead to this path. The family Episcript or Hot Potato is a life Script that gets passed down the family line. It says, "The children in this family carry on the tradition of success and leadership in the family business or profession!" This can be a powerful driver. Likewise a decision by a child to be exactly the opposite of his or her depressed, crazy, alcoholic, or otherwise Loser parents, drives the child into a success-oriented Counterscript life that covers the Script pain during the many years of climb up the ladder of success. This is called Antiscript.

The Red Hot Poker effect carries its subjects through the twenties and thirties, through professional and graduate schools, through the lower levels of business organizations and professional life, probably through marriage, children, and mortgage into advancement and promotion into the middle management levels of organizations. Then something begins to happen, often in the early forties. The initial drive toward success, with its enormous demands on time and energy, begins to bog down as the barriers to further advancement get higher. After all, not everyone can be president—or even vice-president.

At about the same time it seems that **the Red Hot Pokers begin to cool down!** Sandy and Sammy begin to experience a change in their needs. Financial success is well in hand. They have most of the modern appliances needed for comfortable living. The children's educations are well on their way, although financial demands of the college educations require a lot of worry. As the internal drivers begin to cool down, they have a chance to look around at their location in life and they realize that in order to keep up the internal stroking levels and external stroking levels provided by success in achievement they will have to keep on working just as hard for the rest of their lives. They have worked themselves into organizations, where the number of strokes available just for being who they are, is too low to match their needs.

Now they, the mid-level managers, begin to wonder how they got to this place and time, and if indeed their choices are limited. They may get depressed, lose much of their motivation for work, stop identifying so closely with the organization's goals. The organization begins to see them as problem managers. They feel uncomfortable and distracted and the stage is set for Middle-escence, middle years recycling.

Life Begins at 40

In "Childhood and Society"[5] Erikson has described his view of child development through the oral, anal, genital, and latency stages preceding adolescence. Recently, starting with the work of the Schiffs and the Cathexis Institute staff[6] as presented in their workshops, and as presented and extended by Falzett and Maxwell in their booklet **OK Childing and Parenting,**[7] and also with the work of Pam Levin and the staff of Group House as described in her workshops and her booklet **Becoming the Way We Are,**[8] these early stages have been associated with the activation and growth of the use of the various first and second order ego state structures.

The time periods, developmental states, ego states, and major developmental concerns involved in healthy growth are: 0-6 months, early oral, C_1, Natural CHILD, feeding and stroking; 6-18 months, late oral, A_1, Little Professor, exploration; 18 months-3 years, anal, A_2, ADULT ego state, separation; 3-6 years, genital, P_1, Adapted CHILD, imagination, Script writing; 7-10 years, latency, P_2, PARENT ego state, creative activity, arguing. As usual in human affairs, these time periods will vary around these means and may be seriously disrupted by inadequate parenting and other environmental or genetic problems.

Pam Levin has made interesting observations about adolescence,[9] labeling it as a first recycling of the developmental stages. Tasks that were not completed in the early years will be worked on again. Thus at 13 going on 1, if feeding and stroking needs were not adequately met, the young adolescent will again emphasize his or her needs for being fed and held. At 14 going on 2, the adolescent may need to finish breaking the early symbiosis and the family may experience temper tantrums and outbursts of anger again. At 15 going on 3 to 6, the adolescent may be re-evaluating her early Script writings and can change early decisions as she becomes more independent. At 16 to 18 going on 7 to 10, there may be a lot of arguing about values as the adolescent re-evaluates what he has incorporated into his PARENT.

The phenomenon of Middle-escence seems to have this same quality of recycling and the phrase "Life Begins at 40" signals the beginning of another recycling for the group of one time Achievers and present time dispirited middle managers.

As adolescence begins around thirteen years, plus or minus two or three years, so the time of middle-escence recycling varies from forty, but most managers with whom this concept has been discussed identify the years between thirty-five and forty-five as years of change, re-evaluation, and new beginnings. The Red Hot Pokers of youth have cooled down and Sandy's and Sammy's focus on stroking needs has begun to turn from internal stroking to external, and they begin to attempt to solve relationship problems which were incompletely and unsatisfactorily solved in childhood and adolescence.

Thus the process begins anew. At 40 going on 1, body needs take a new and important emphasis. Finding new restaurants, tasting wines and cheeses, learning about gourmet cooking, tuning up the body, getting massages, learning tennis, and sexual swinging. Feeding and stroking are re-explored.

Then comes 45 going on 2. Sammy and/or Sandy begin to struggle within the symbiotic relationships that they have set up in their marriages and/or in the life enveloping corporation to which they have dedicated the last ten or fifteen years of work and association. They feel tied down, furious at the restraints. Anger and frustration break out as they attempt to explore anew to find ways to be independent, to think for themselves, to make their own choices, and to be able to do this without being abandoned by their stroke suppliers.

At 50 going on 3 to 6, Script writing and early Script decisions again come into prominence. The middle-escent, having re-explored and tried out some new sources of stroking and feeding, and having gotten through the scare of breaking or beginning to break symbiotic chains, now begins to re-evaluate his or her whole life style. Perhaps he is back in therapy, rewriting his Script, redeciding, getting internal permission in place of injunctions—do's and be's, in place of don't and you'd better's. She may be in therapy or in a women's consciousness raising group to break her banal Script. He or they may be getting cured of alcoholic or suicidal life Scripts, going from tragic to winner's Scripting. This is a time to change life positions, time structure, stroking patterns and all of the other changes that go with Script change.

Finally, there is 55 going on 7 to 10, when people often take one more look at their basic value systems and sort out what part of their PARENT ego state is still appropriate and which needs to be set aside in favor of new values more effective and suitable to the here-and-now of the middle-escent. This is often a time when religious values are looked at again and perhaps re-activated. At this age the philosophical Why becomes more important. Why are we here? What's it all about? What's the purpose been of my life? What is the relevance of the profit system to the quality of life on the earth?

As with the early developmental stages and the adolescent recycling, not everyone will be able to get what they need, and may find themselves shunted or shoved aside and labeled "Dead-wood." Thus early Winners may end up as late Losers.

Deadwood

Old Achievers never die. They become "Deadwood." This is the label often applied to demotivated, distracted, unstroked, low-productivity, middle-level managers once known and recognized for exactly the opposite traits. The time structure in the work situation of a manager now labeled as "Deadwood" would likely look as shown in Figure 51.

FIGURE 51
Time structure of Deadwood versus Livewood

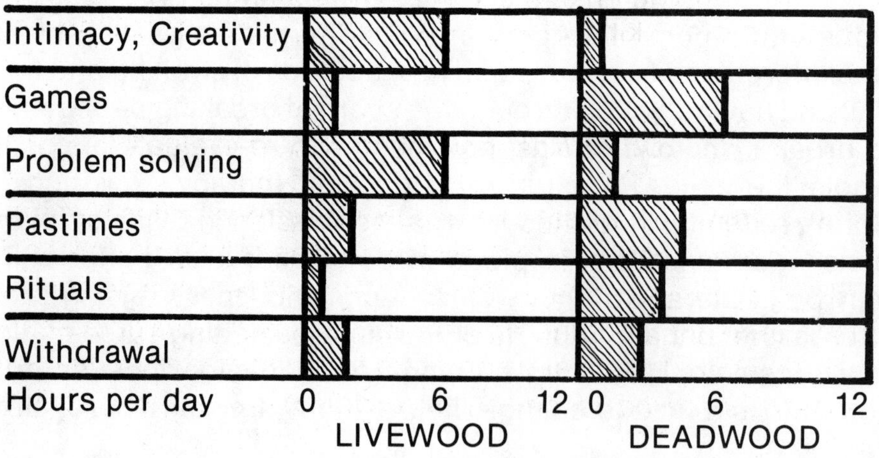

	LIVEWOOD	DEADWOOD
Intimacy, Creativity		
Games		
Problem solving		
Pastimes		
Rituals		
Withdrawal		
Hours per day	0 6 12	0 6 12

When the time structure of an executive in an organization begins to show the changes indicated in Figure 51, he or she is traditionally watched more and more closely, and then is likely to be "gotten rid of," "kicked upstairs," shunted aside into some non-sensitive position, or pushed into early retirement. In a management dominated by self-motivating achievers, no other options seem feasible. After all they are still "cutting the mustard." Why can't Sammy run any more? If he has been around too long to fire, "let's make him a director or something, to get him out of the way, and bring in some young blood."

The costs of this seemingly neat system for dealing with the situation can be very large. First, the organization loses the very large investment in time and experience involved in training an executive. Then there are all the costly years of his inefficiency and low productivity, while the organization is watching and deciding to do something if the situation gets bad enough. Also there is a morale factor. "If after all those good years this company kicks Sandy out just like that, or otherwise humiliates her, do I really want to work for such a heartless bunch?"

The TA approach to human problem solving from an—"I'm OK. You're OK. Let's get on with it"—approach offers an important alternative. TA re-education is aimed at providing clients a structure within which they can redecide to be Winners instead of Almost-Winners or Losers. Thus the TA approach provides effective structures for remotivating and renewing ex-achievers in a non-scripted way so that they can recognize their needs and learn ways to satisfy them. This, of course, may include getting into some other kind of work, non-work, or organization, in an OK way.

Remotivation, Renewal and Regrowth

Often the hardest part of solving a problem lies in defining the problem. After that the possibilities for solution come easier. At this point in a typical workshop on middle-escence there will be many heads nodding agreement, and many participants will be ready to begin to make contracts for change along lines which they are prepared to devise, in order to solve their particular problems.

163

The principal problem in working with management and other organizational groups is to provide a structure for change and problem solving with adequate protection and an effective but low confrontation level. In this situation, where typically there is no therapy contract, the participants can learn and redecide at a comfortable anxiety level so that they will not be scared away and the project dropped.

A very useful structure to meet these problems is the often used one of collecting data from the group either on large news-print sheets which can then be posted around the room to stimulate further work and thought or to have the individual group members collect the data in their own minds, or write it down. This is followed by sharing and discussion of their findings in groups of 2 to 6, and then discussion in the large group where the leader can proceed to clarify and negotiate clear contracts.

As in treatment groups, the general plan for change involves discovery of Script injunctions, early decisions, and the resulting destructive adapted behaviors, working up to and through the impasses of redecision, implementing and reinforcing new and more satisfying behavior patterns.

The problem of homeostasis, the pressure for equilibrium, which makes change difficult in the family as members attempt to keep each other from disturbing the status quo even though the situation is lousy for all, can be even more formidable in an organization which exerts so much financial pressure on its members. Thus in organizational work a large part of the effort needs to be applied to changing the organizational environment, particularly along the lines of stroking levels and protection available.

Application and Exercises

A sequence of questions and fantasies that can serve as a fabric for small and large group sharing, discussion, and redecision are as follows:

1. Where are you now in your middle-escence recycling?
2. Write down the Red Hot Poker injunctions and Counterscript instructions that you use to run your life.

164

3. Fantasy a conversation between your Adapted CHILD and your Natural CHILD around the conflict of wants, needs, and shoulds that goes on in you.

4. Write down a list of changes in your needs in recent years compared to your needs in the 20's.

5. Make a time structure plot for your working time as it is now and as it was in your 20's.

6. Make a time structure plot for a "Deadwood" manager that you know of, work with, or supervise.

7. What are the stroking levels and stroking sources in your organization?

8. Discuss life planning—one hour to many days' duration for this exercise. Categories for examination and writing include major areas of your life; where are you now in these areas; where do you want to be; what resources do you need to make the changes; what is your time schedule?

9. What changes will need to be made in your organization's structure in order to allow remotivation, renewal, and regrowth for its middle-escent problem managers?

At some point in a consultation, the managers begin to consider major changes in the organizational structures. This is then a problem in organizational development which requires considerable cost over the years in time and money. Although strokes don't cost anything, the time involved in stroking does cost, and an organization that relies on making a profit in order to exist, will need some evidence of results to support this expense, for example, a demonstration of reduced turnover rate for its managers and staff.

As in the long run the CHILD runs the show, this program for change will need to be aimed at providing more positive stroking, excitement, opportunities for creativity and play for the manager. Changes contracted for by the individual and the organization may include re-education, re-assignment, setting up new programs and projects, or relocation out of the organization in an OK way.

REFERENCES

1. Berne, E. **What Do You Say After You Say Hello?** Grove Press, New York, 1972, pp. 203–206.
2. Kahler, T. and Capers, H. "The Miniscript," **Transactional Analysis Journal,** IV:1, January 1974, pp. 26–42.
3. English, F. "Episcript and the 'Hot Potato' Game," **Transactional Analysis Bulletin,** VIII:32, October 1969, pp. 77–82.
4. Berne, E. **What Do You Say After You Say Hello?** pp. 132–133, 171–172.
5. Erikson, E. **Childhood and Society.** Norton and Co., New York 1963, pp. 49–108.
6. Schiff, J. et al. **Cathexis Reader.** Harper and Row, New York, 1975.
7. Maxwell, J. and Falzett, B. **OK Childing and Parenting.** Transactional Analysis Institute of El Paso, El Paso, 1974.
8. Levin, P. **Becoming the Way We Are.** Group House, Berkeley, 1974.
9. Ibid and private communications.

Chapter Ten:
PLANNING FOR CHANGE

Goals and Objectives

The first step in the process of change is to decide what the desirable objectives are.[1] Many people when asked "What do you want to change?" answer "I don't know." This is usually a way of saying that they won't say or don't trust their inner feelings about what they really want; however, people really **do** know what they want and can say very clearly. This is one of the first objectives in Transactional Analysis counseling or consulting: to find out what the person wants and needs, and set about helping the client solve the problems standing in his or her way.

The same is true with organizations—the first job of change is to find out from the collective CHILD what are the important goals. Where do you want this organization to be some time from now? What are the most important changes to be made? What are the desirable directions for growth? What changes in you or in the organization would bring renewed enthusiasm, excitement, and creativity?

As the CHILD and the intuitive Little Professor live with fantasy and magical ideas, the first stated objectives are likely to be far from reality in some cases. The creative spirit of the CHILD is often connected with fantasy, as the creative leap is not made by calculation, but by intuition and a reordering of facts in new and unpredictable ways. It is for this reason that brainstorming sessions have a rule against criticism of ideas while they are being collected. The CHILD will turn off in the face of the Critical PARENT.

The first choice of objectives is the ideal or image of the future. When this image is out in the open, then the reality testing and probability computing capabilities of the ADULT can be put

167

to use to figure out which objectives have a good enough chance of being reached; then problem-solving can be brought into the reality level.

The Process of Change

WHAT IS CHANGE?

Change means doing something different from what has been done before. People develop characteristic ways of getting strokes for themselves. These characteristic ways depend on their life styles which arise in early years from PARENTal injunctions. Decisions based upon these injunctions are made according to acceptable ways of getting needs and wants filled. Depending upon the intensity with which the early injunctions were imposed, the CHILD settles upon a Script that is more or less rigid and therefore which can be more or less easily changed or rewritten. When people grow up they carry these old tape recordings in their heads as PARENT ego states and continually reinforce the old behavior with great emotional intensity. It is for this reason that change is so difficult. The person must proceed with new behavior and face the fear of threats and criticism from his own PARENT until the new behavior is established and reinforced by positive stroking, and the anxiety due to old Critical PARENT messages has died away.

Growth stops as a result of script limitations. As choices are limited due to injunctions, a person's life is also limited and growth can stop at one or another stage. Breaking with Script rigidity then allows the personality to continue its development and to explore new areas for creativity, self expression, and self motivation.

WHY CHANGE?

In an individual or in an organization the questions the CHILD or the collective CHILD will be asking are "Why change? What will I get out of change?" Since change and further growth means risk and disapproval from PARENT tapes, the CHILD will want to know and see what he is getting before he wants to give

168

up old and even destructive ways of behaving. This is why immediate positive stroking of changed behavior is so important for
permanent change.

POTENCY, PERMISSION AND PROTECTION

Change requires the presence of three factors: potency,
permission, and protection. Potency refers to the effectiveness,
credibility, and trust afforded to a leader, consultant, or counselor.
It is similar to the potency acknowledged by children toward their
parents. A parent or a potent leader can give permission for a
person to change and break with the past. A potent leader gives
permission and also offers protection against the fear of risk and
change. This is especially important in breaking injunctions and
changing life styles, as this kind of change goes against the person's traditional way of getting what he needs (learned in his
original family). Learning to be open about feelings or to trust or
to feel OK about self and others, can be a very frightening process
and the person needs protection while he is changing. (See Figure 52.)

Protection is a crucial factor in bringing about change.
Organizational change can bring many changes in the lives of
the management and staff. Communication patterns are changed;
working relationships are changed; jobs are changed or elim-
inated. There is much threat to the usual way of life. If staff feel
that their fears and personal concerns are also a concern of the
management, then resistance to change will decrease. If not,
then resistance to change, in one or more of its many forms,
will grow and seriously interfere with or prevent any significant
change. Without change, growth is impeded.

CHANGE AND RENEWAL

Renewal implies a change in direction of growth that has
slowed down or has been decreasing, usually due to lack of interest and motivation, in other words, the rate and availability of
stroking has been lacking or decreasing. Renewal means finding
new sources of strokes and making new decisions to seek strokes
from new people, new situations, and new work.

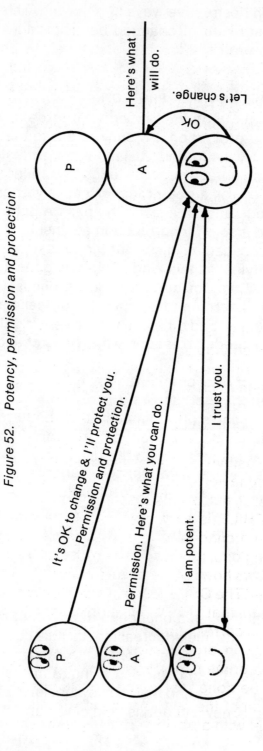

Figure 52. Potency, permission and protection

170

THE IMPASSE

When an individual (or a group or an organization) decides on change and begins to make the change, the phenomenon of the impasse or resistance soon begins to become apparent. All sorts of reasons against the change arise in the people's heads emanating from their PARENT ego state. The CHILD gets scared because this new behavior is opposed to the way he or she was stroked to behave when young. At the impasse the person may suddenly feel scared, may turn off his feelings, or may get angry and refuse to go further. The internal conflict is PARENT-CHILD. The job of the consultant, therapist, counselor, or facilitator is to lead the participants to the impasse, to let them become aware of the inner conflict, and to stand by with support and protection from PARENT anger at breaking injunctions. In an organization, resistance is often based on fear of losing one's position or privileges; if trust levels are low, the collective CHILD will strongly resist change.

If the CHILD is offered protection and accepts it, it will begin to dare to change and try new directions. This is the beginning of breaking through the impasse. At this point, the CHILD needs permission to change and also needs protection and support, not only against external dangers, but also against the inner terror brought about by old PARENTal injunctions. An important support of change is the presence of immediate positive stroking. Positive stroking encourages the CHILD to adopt new ways of behavior. Otherwise why should anyone change? What do they get out of this discomfort and pain and inconvenience? The CHILD is very practical. Even though the person may be offered a change from a negative stroking position to a positive stroking one, he may refuse. After all he is used to being kicked and knows how it feels and he doesn't know how the positive strokes feel. The CHILD doesn't want to give up anything, not even a situation that may seem unpleasant to someone else, especially if this corresponds to his Script style.

Similarly, in organizations where negative stroking has been used as a prime motivating method, the change to positive stroking must be done slowly and with the permission, consent, and cooperation of the staff. As the advantages and better feelings associated with a positive stroking atmosphere become ap-

171

parent, further change will be less resisted. This situation has been described by Peter Drucker[2] for the case of IBM, where change was no longer resisted once the staff had become convinced that the company policy was to preserve employment.

TIME

A major factor in growth, change, and renewal is time. People cannot and will not change overnight. They may make a decision to change at any moment, but the change will not be permanent and self-perpetuating until a new feedback system has been established, whereby the person is getting strokes for the new behavior and thus is encouraged to repeat such behavior so as to get more strokes, and so on. In the case of individuals, this time is characteristically several weeks to several months. In an organization where many people must change, the process requires several years to become permanent. For this reason, organizational change must be planned and continued over three to five years, if a permanent effect is desired. Decisions for change can be made in a one, two, or several day workshop, but much time is required to build the changes into a new organizational pattern of behavior.

During this time of change, the environment must be watched, so that new impasses are brought out into the open as they arise and decisions made in a continuous fashion. If the environment becomes hostile, for example, via a depression or recession, the organization will need to organize its resources for new markets and new income so that the staff is protected during change; otherwise it will become scared and retreat into defensive positions and old Script life styles, which are likely to be unproductive and rigid.

Using Transactional Analysis for Change, Renewal, and Growth

The Transactional Analysis theory is designed for simplified understanding of human behavior, and the application of the theory in groups is aimed toward change instead of mere understanding. Understanding of one's miserable situation does not help. How we can change our lives in order to get more of what we want and enjoy, is a style of getting on with life no matter how difficult the situation.

The goal of Transactional Analysis is to help Losers, Almost-Losers, and Almost-Winners change as much towards the Winner's position as they want to go. The desire of the person himself to want to change is a crucial rule to follow. No one will change unless he or she wants to.

These same rules for change can be applied to organizations. Unless the top management of the organization becomes committed to change, nothing will happen—short of revolution, of course.

PROCESS FOR CHANGE

Two of the most important procedures for change either with individuals or groups are: first, the giving of ADULT information concerning human relationships; second, the analysis of human relationships via the transactions occurring. Along with this, the group members are taught the elements of Script theory, how injunctions are converted into a life style, about positive and negative strokes, about time structure, and life positions. This information usually gets applied to the members' own lives, either in open discussion or in the process of absorbing and thinking about the meaning of the TA personality model, for themselves and the people with whom they come into contact.

CONTRACTS

The next part of the procedure lies in the application of the theory to the lives of the group members and to their daily interactions with other staff members. Where there are difficulties, the theory points out alternate ways of proceeding, and facilitates setting up contracts for change which can be connected easily to the overall goals of the organization and to long-range planning efforts. As the main difficulty in long-range planning lies in the resistance to change arising from fear of change, the process can be approached by a series of contracts for change in a piece-meal fashion. Some typical contracts are: to keep the Critical PARENT turned off and stay in the ADULT; to give positive strokes; to ask for positive strokes; to give positive strokes to oneself for a job well done; to express feelings of fear or anger openly; to not discount a problem or a person; to avoid Games by turning on the ADULT at the critical moment; to take risks of trust; to take care of oneself—by working less, drinking less, smoking less, sleeping more, and so on.

These are a few typical contracts for change that usually arise in any group of people and are basic to developing good relationships and improved decision-making capabilities. Some of the changes required in order to achieve change, renewal, and growth in an organization are:

1. Improved decision-making by ADULT contact with reality uncontaminated by CHILD fantasy and fear.
2. Increased basic trust.
3. Increased positive stroking.
4. Separation of ADULT decision-making from PARENTal prejudice and rigidity.
5. Clarified and mutually agreed upon goals.
6. Openness of communication.

TA training and organizational change can be carried out in individual interviews, in groups of five to twelve, or in classes of forty, sixty or one hundred. The work can be taught on an educational basis, on a counseling basis, on an intellectual level, or on an experiential level. The choice of approach depends upon the needs and desires of the organization and the level of involvement desired.

Because change in human behavior has a high emotional content, change, renewal, and growth will be more rapid when there is an experiential involvement as well as an intellectual commitment.

Designing the Future

The past is finished, and with sufficient records we can know what happened. The present is happening, and we can experience these events and feelings now, providing we are tuned in to ourselves and to others. The future will happen as an extension and consequence of the events of the past and present, with uncertainty added from the natural randomness of nature. By the use of planning, we can certainly influence future events, but it's a good idea to remember the limitations in this influence brought about by the inevitability of unexpected and chance events. The farther that we attempt to plan into the future, the more uncertain will be the resemblance between our plans and actual events that will occur.

This concept of uncertainty is more easily understood and accepted by the ADULT than by the CHILD ego states. If the ADULT has said to the CHILD, "we will go to get an ice cream soda this afternoon," and then the car breaks down, the bus drivers go on strike, or there is a power failure so that all of the ice cream in town melts, still the CHILD will say, "But you promised!" The CHILD lives in the here-and-now and does not have an effective contact with concepts of time and the uncertainties of the real world.

Thus disappointment, disillusionment, and rejection of the planning process, occur and will continue to occur in organizations where CHILD impatience and fantasy are not adequately counterbalanced by ADULT thinking, and effective, appropriate PARENT values and experience from the past.

BASIC DECISIONS

Before beginning a planning process there are some vital basic decisions that need to be made.

First, there must be a decision on the part of the responsible management to make a commitment to the discipline required for consistent ongoing planning, and to the cost in time and manpower devoted to the planning process.

Second, there must be an understanding and a separation of the mechanisms for long-range (two or more years in the future), intermediate-range (one or two years), and short-range (less than one year) planning from day-to-day problem solving and putting out fires.

Third, there must be available structures whereby problem solving can be separated into personal CHILD feeling-level problems and into ADULT business consequence-level problems.

Fourth, there must be provided, via internal or external consultants, adequate permission and protection for planners to express their fears and resentments along with other feelings, so that CHILD creativity will not be turned off by a Little Professor decision that this is not a safe place in which to take risks.

THE PLANNING PROCESS

The literature on organizational change is full of various approaches to planning. Some of the most important elements in the planning process as seen from the TA theory of human behavior are the following:

▶ *THE IMAGE OF THE FUTURE.* The main question is, "Where do we want to go?" This may be tempered with "where can we or where should we go?" but in order to mobilize the energy of the CHILD towards the goals of the organization, a first requirement is to obtain a vision of the ideal future, as fantasied by the CHILD ego states of the planners and participants in the organization. This image is obtained by free brainstorming via Little Profesor and Natural CHILD, in order to gather an uncensored and unevaluated list of the ideal qualities of the organization at some specified time in the future. It is essential that Critical PARENT as well as evaluating ADULT be kept turned off during this process.

▶ *SEPARATION OF PERSONAL AND BUSINESS IMAGES.* Separation of these two images will help the focus of the images, as seen by the feeling level and the creative levels of the plan-

176

ners. The differences on this level will probably pinpoint likely areas of conflict and disagreement in later planning stages. The personal image of the future will represent the wants and needs of the CHILD in the individual. The business image will represent the goals and needs of the organization for its survival and growth or continued health, and will have more ADULT and PARENTal content.

Conflicts and differences between the viewpoints and frame of reference of the CHILD, with its large component of focus on stroking and other basic necessities of life, and the viewpoints and frames of reference of the ADULT and PARENT ego states, with the ADULT contact with reality and the PARENT contact with the experience of the past, are of major importance in individual changes of life style. They can be expected to be even more important and more difficult to resolve in an organization made up of many individuals with differing needs, frames of reference, and so on.

If these differences are accepted and treated as natural and normal, and not discounted and treated as abnormal, then the likelihood of the appearance of compliance, passivity, and rebellion from Adapted CHILD positions will be reduced. Otherwise, the appearance of resistance (in other words, resistance to change) will reduce or render ineffective programs for organizational change.

▶ *SETTING OF PRIORITIES.* A next important stage is voting or otherwise coming to a consensus, on the priority rank of the various parts of the Image of the Future, in both the personal and business sides. As many of the staff members as possible need to be involved in this voting so that the priority list reflects the feelings, thoughts, and opinions of the people who must do the work and put in the energy necessary to carry out the program. A sense of participation strokes people for their ADULTs and increases trust in the final decision-makers. ADULT and PARENT ego states begin to be used at this stage as well as CHILD. This process illustrates the ongoing nature of planning, as the

177

priorities will change with time, and an organization will need to continuously re-examine its priorities so that it doesn't get stuck with an outdated set of products, procedures, personnel, or anything else.

► *ADULT EVALUATION.* Now the planning group must begin to examine the items of the idealized goal. Figure 53 shows schematically the progression of the planning process. The horizontal axis represents time, past to the left and future to the right. NOW, is at the axis intersection. Without any planning, the organization will be carried into the future, influenced by daily decision making and by randomly and accidentally occurring events. At some time in the future, T, the organization will be somewhere, perhaps prospering, perhaps extinct. This is labeled by the arrow on the time axis. If an ideal image is constructed in the planning process, this will represent a vision of the desired future, and is shown as the jagged outlined areas in the personal and business fields. In fact, the organization may not end up anywhere near the ideal image, but at least it has an idea of where it wants to go and thus has some chance to influence its future in an organized way.

ADULT evaluation of the planning items now allows a look at the feasibility, cost, desirability, and the like of each item. The ADULT is able to make good contact with reality and to lower the priority of items that seem less likely to be within range of success, or that seem to involve too much risk for the organization, or that seem undesirable for any other well-based reason.

The result of this evaluation is an ADULT evaluated image of the future and is likely to look considerably different from the first image. These images are shown by the smoothly outlined areas in Figure 53

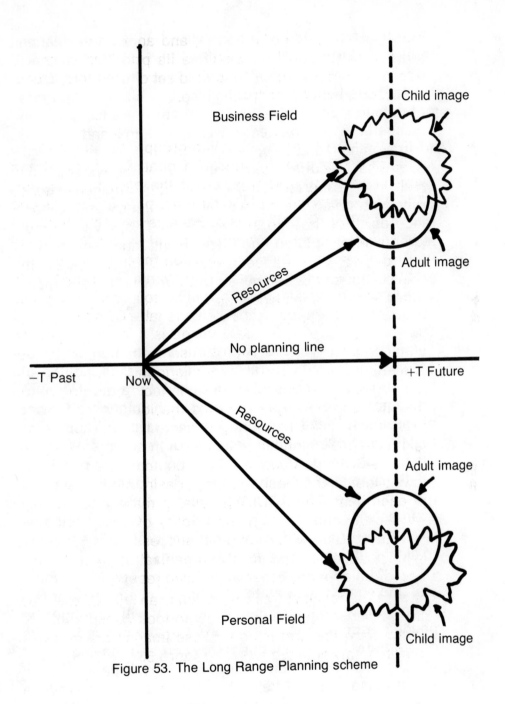

Figure 53. The Long Range Planning scheme

► *PARENT EVALUATION.* It is also a good idea to look at the images from a Nurturing or Protective PARENT point of view, as well as from a Critical PARENT view. The contrast between these two viewpoints will again indicate what parts of the management PARENTal structure are likely to run into conflicts with the needs, wants, feelings, and creative energy of the CHILD.

   The Nurturing and Protective value systems will result in a further shaping of the future images. These processes again emphasize the usefulness and importance of all of the ego states. PARENT is a very useful storehouse of opinion and instructions, and, rather than discard PARENT, the idea in Transactional Analysis is to separate out and decommission the destructive and inappropriate parts of this ego state.

► *DEVELOPMENT OF RESOURCES.* At this point in the planning process, which may have taken some weeks or months of regular meetings to solidify, there will be a great deal of agreement as to the future desired by the planners. It's not necessary to have agreement on all issues. Those that remain controversial can be set aside for further work on the next planning go-around. Now the concrete problems are those related to bringing the plan into reality, and the question of resources comes into prominence. What resources will be needed; where will they come from; how will they be organized; what new structures will be needed to aid the utilization of the new resources?

   What additional personnel will be needed? Which staff members will need to be shifted or retrained for different responsibilities? How much staff will no longer be needed or be able to be supported by the changed goals or programs? How will this relocation and moving out of the organization be done in an OK and humane way? How will stroking rates be kept at high levels so as to reduce the anxieties and fear of the CHILD during the change period, until new programs and stroking patterns are established?

180

If new funds will be needed for the planned changes, where will the funds come from? How much money will be available for personnel problems mentioned in the previous paragraph? Most organizations are aware of the costs for new facilities but are not or have not recognized the essential costs for staff readjustment to change. A new piece of equipment, plus an angry or passive operator, means poor efficiency, at least, and resistance, union problems, and strikes, as some of the escalated results of ignoring CHILD needs, wants, and fears.

When the change process begins, a number of problems can be expected to appear regularly. An essential structure for organizational change is problem-solving groups, committees, or whatever they might be labeled. These are small (six to fifteen), participant meetings, at which both ADULT and CHILD confrontation can take place in a safe and protected atmosphere. Many of these structures are in use by consultants trained in the various modes of organizational development, including Transactional Analysis. The structure needs to be designed and made to fit the particular problems of the particular organization. Trust levels need to be established between the planners and their consultant. CHILD fears need to be expressed and taken into consideration. Then, ADULT problem solving can proceed in an effective manner.

► *MOVING INTO THE FUTURE.* Time passes quickly when the planning process and its subsidiary problems begin to grow. Plans that were several years from realization suddenly are only two years or one year away! The long-range planning moves into the intermediate-, short-range, and then the day-to-day planning schedule. The organization will need other structures to handle these events as they move into the present, and meanwhile the long-range planners must keep on with their three, five, seven, or even more years planning of the future. The process does not stop as long as the organization wishes to remain viable, and so the planning process becomes an integral part of organiza-

181

tional life, with all of the problem-solving structures being continuously renewed, revised, replaced, and rewarded.

With an effective long-range planning program, the organization's executives and managers can feel that their lives need not be just one daily round of putting out fires and running the operation by the seat of their pants. They can put some planning into their own lives so that they can be effective for the organization, and also maintain their own stroking structures in family and social life, so that they will not run into the Middle-escence blues.

Application and Exercises

Carry out the following planning exercises for your organization: business, school, clinic, club, social organization, team, church, temple, golf-foursome, family, or whatever.

1. Who are the responsible people that must make the decision in order for this planning program to become a reality?
2. For what time are you planning in the future? An estimate of time necessary to change an organization is:

Less than 25 people	1 year or less
100 or less	2 years
1000 or less	3 to 4 years
More than 1000	4 or more years

3. What are your resources for outside or inside consultants, counselors, and the like, should they be needed?
4. List the kinds of protections that the CHILD in your organization needs. How will you provide each of these protections?
5. Make a list of the ideal qualities that your organization would have in the future, (timed according to your answer in question 2), assuming that it will be the perfect place for you. Include at least twenty items. Do this from your Little Professor. Keep PARENT and ADULT turned off.

182

6. Divide the items in question 5 into two lists, one for items that relate to how you will feel as part of the organization, and another that relates to how effectively the organization is operating and maintaining its viability.
7. Order the lists according to your CHILD's priority, Natural CHILD or Little Professor (Adult in the CHILD), if only one person is doing this exercise. If a number of people are voting, allow each person to vote for one-third of the items.
8. Evaluate the lists with your ADULT in terms of the reality of expecting the item to be accomplished. Eliminate items or reduce the priority rank of items that seem out of contact with reality.
9. Evaluate the lists with your Nurturing and Protective PARENT, eliminating items or reducing the priority rank of items that run counter to your value system or to the community value system, in amounts that would be destructive for you or others. (The items to be considered here for elimination would be those that might be positions taken by a rebellious, Adapted CHILD, rather than a person willing to fight for what he considers to be right).
10. For each item on the lists, consider what resources will be needed in terms of personnel changes, funds required, protection, and so on; anything that will be required in order to support, facilitate, or encourage the reaching of the item goal.
11. For each item on the list, consider how the organization might interfere or frustrate reaching the goal, and what problems are likely to arise which will need to be solved.
12. How do you feel about your organization after completing this series of exercises, as contrasted with your feelings before you started?
13. What decisions will you make about carrying out this planning project?

REFERENCES

1. Bennett, T. Many of the important ideas on long-range planning in this chapter are by private communication during a year-long seminar on organizational development at George Williams College in 1971–72.
2. Drucker, P. **The Practice of Management**, Harper and Row, New York, 1954.
3. Berne, E. **What Do You Say After You Say Hello?** Grove Press, New York, 1972, Chapter 11.

III.
Evaluation

Chapter Eleven:
EVALUATION OF STAFF PERFORMANCE

*Evaluation of Staff Performance in Defining and
Reaching Objectives Using Transactional Analysis*

What are the variables that must be monitored in order to test the effectiveness of the TA approach to management training? How is it possible to tell if change is occurring and if it is in the desired direction? What kinds of data are necessary and how shall this data be collected?

This chapter presents a discussion of the problem: How to tell if the TA approach to management problems discussed in Chapters One through Ten is working.

The ideas presented would need to be worked out in detail with the Transactional Analysis organizational consultant as the ideas given here are only in outline. Quantitative methods for measurement and evaluation do not yet exist for TA theory. Most of the procedures are based on clinical and teaching experience. Opportunities for research in this field are wide open and the relatively clear independent variables presented by Transactional Analysis theory offer many clear directions.

*Validity and Accuracy of Information Exchange:
Chapter One and Two*

ANALYSIS OF TRANSACTIONS
The first general area to be checked is that of communication. This was the general problem considered in Chapters One and Two. What kinds of transactions are going on? This data can be obtained by third parties either by listening at conferences and meetings or wherever management-staff communication is going on, and by examining memos and other written communications sent throughout the organization.

187

What ego states are heard from most frequently? Does management speak primarily from its PARENT, ADULT, or CHILD? Where are the statements aimed? Are they PARENT to PARENT, PARENT to CHILD, PARENT to ADULT, ADULT to ADULT, or what? What kind of responses are most frequent: PARENT to PARENT, CHILD to PARENT, ADULT to ADULT, CHILD to CHILD?

These transactions can be sorted out by using the verbal, gesture, and word type clues described in Chapter One.

How many of the management are speaking primarily from one ego state to the exclusion of the others? An autocratic management would primarily come on PARENT and the staff is expected to respond primarily from the CHILD position. Does the management have an over-abundance of PARENTal types or do they switch appropriately between all ego states?

What is the rate of occurrence of straight complementary transactions as compared to ulterior double messages or angular transactions? How many crossed transactions occur at meetings and conferences leading to crossed transactions and the breaking off of communication via game playing with its payoff of negative strokes and the saving up of brown stamps or grudges for later return?

How do these types of communication occur among the staff? As parents in the home set the style for children, so the communication style of the management will set the style for the staff—at least overtly. If the management communication style is quite different from the staff style then there is likely to be much ulterior communication in order to cover up true feelings.

STROKING LEVELS

What are the stroking level and the stroking ratio between positive and negative strokes? This can be measured by third party observation at meetings, conferences, and at informal discussions. Stroking levels can also be determined by checking with management and staff. People are usually aware of the kind of strokes that they seek or receive. These two methods of measurement will be expected to agree, providing trust levels are high enough so that straight information is given. Quantitative measurement of stroke intensity is difficult as some strokes feel more important than others and strokes from a peer may feel less weighty than strokes from a high management officer. The use of stroking ratios helps eliminate the problem of defining accurate stroke measurement.

BASIC TRUST

Collection of accurate information undistorted by fear and anger depends upon the trust level existing in the organization. Trust level can be measured by observing the occurrence of CHILD communications—which are usually on the emotional level. As trust level increases, both staff and management will feel safe in revealing their emotional state and feelings. On the contrary, in a low trust level atmosphere, communication will be primarily from ADULT or PARENT levels since this is safer. A simple measure of CHILD communication can be obtained by merely walking around in the offices and corridors and listening to the sound level. Low trust will result in a very quiet atmosphere while a high and excited noise level indicates much CHILD communication.

ADULT OPERATION

Presence or change in levels of effective ADULT operation can be measured by the number of decisions taken at meetings. ADULT effectiveness will also be inversely proportional to the amount of time spent in Rituals (worrying about the agenda, parliamentary procedures, and so on), Pastimes (vacations, General Motors—What car are you driving now?, Martini—6/1 or 15/1, or Ain't It Awful), and Games. A simple check of ADULT effectiveness can be made in the last few minutes of a meeting by taking a poll of the members as to their estimate of the fraction of time that they were operating out of their ADULT.

PARENT OPERATION

Percentage of Critical or Rescuing PARENT operation versus Protective or Nurturing PARENT operation can be measured by the amount of time spent in crossed transactions, arguments, put downs, defensiveness, and scapegoating, or rescuing in contrast to protection, setting of moral standards, support, giving advice that is asked for, and acceptance. Again, a third party consultant observer at meetings is the best way to measure this quantity.

Effectiveness of the Interview System: Chapter Three

ANALYSIS OF THE INTERVIEW TRANSACTIONS

The effectiveness of the interview system is measured from both the interviewer and candidate viewpoint. Information can be obtained by third party interviews or by a checklist questionnaire.

The first important question is: What kind of transactions were occurring during the interview? Were they all ADULT-ADULT or was there CHILD-CHILD, CHILD-PARENT, PARENT-CHILD, and so on? What was the ratio of these various types of transactions? Was there a great deal of non-verbal communication? Were there many ulterior transactions or angular transactions? How many crossed transactions occurred?

What was the trust and openness level as indicated by the internal feelings and comfort level of the participants? What was the corresponding level of CHILD communication of feelings? Did the person feel safe with CHILD communication or was this seen as risky? Did it elicit PARENT response from the other person?

How do the participants think or feel about the interview as expressed by each of their own ego states? Each ego state will probably have a different estimate of the interview and the other person as well as the performance of their own self. These questions will be connected with the Script messages carried by each person and the tendency to project feelings onto the other party. An interviewer who consistently finds the same objectionable qualities in a series of applicants, is likely to be projecting his own Script concepts onto the other person and will be distorting the reality of the interview.

EXCLUDING EGO STATES

What ego state made the decision to hire or not to hire,

and to accept or not to accept the offer? Is the interviewer making decisions from his CHILD exclusively or from his PARENT or is there a large contribution of ADULT probability calculation? CHILD intuition and PARENTal tradition are important to listen to, but if the decisions are being dominated by CHILD fantasy or by PARENTal prejudice then the results of interviewing are likely to be poor.

SCRIPT EFFECTS

The ego state that is most important in making the decision will have a considerable effect on the type of personnel hired. For example, if the Critical PARENT of the interviewer is dominating, it is likely that the person hired will have turned on an Adapted CHILD which suits this PARENT. In this case the relationship has started out as PARENT-CHILD and the new staff members are less likely to be persons who will develop into independent operators but will always be looking to the Boss for direction. If the CHILD has made the decision, then fantasy and wishful thinking may have dominated reality testing and the staff will likely show signs of unconcern for reality. Particularly in new and rapidly growing organizations, this can lead to disaster from lack of planning and fiscal controls.

PREDICTIVE VALIDITY

Confirmation of the predictions of the TA theory can be made by rechecking with the original interview information after six and twelve months. How do the various ego states of the interviewer and the new employee feel now about the candidate and the job?

Change in Organizations and Effectiveness of Management: Chapters Four through Ten

DATA FROM MANAGEMENT EGO STATES

Following the sequence of Chapters Four through Ten on management of personnel, the first thing to evaluate is whether management is getting its needs and wants satisfied, that is, What does management's CHILD think about what is going on

191

in the organization? Then, what are its ADULT estimates of the organization's development? And finally, does its PARENT think that the organization is meeting commitments and obligations to its traditions and to the society and culture that it lives in?

The separation of all such estimates into PARENT, ADULT, and CHILD estimates clarifies and sorts out the information. This avoids confusing overlap between material that has to do with emotional content (CHILD), here-and-now content (ADULT), and the past (PARENT).

► *EGO STATE OBJECTIVES.* Setting and reaching objectives is a prime management function. The evaluation of this function is dependent upon the existence of long-range (three to five years) planning so that a set of objectives chosen from the point of view of all three ego states has been clearly set out. Periodically the situation with regard to reaching or approaching the objectives can be checked. This checking can be carried out via third party interviewing at the top management level and by questionnaire for other more highly population management levels. In order that the CHILD not get bored with such questionnaires, they had better be short and clear, and the information obtained from them fed back promptly to the management at as high a stroking level as possible.

The same measurements are of value in the staff's estimate of satisfaction of its needs and wants as listed in Chapter Three.

PARENT, ADULT, and CHILD evaluation of the effectiveness of management can provide valuable feedback to management. As staff should also be involved in the long-range planning efforts, they will be able to evaluate independently from their own P, A, and C viewpoints, what objectives have been reached and how the organization is doing on the necessary problem-solving, organizational change and planning, in order to reach objectives not yet achieved. Staff interviewing or questionnaires can provide accurate estimates of the stroking levels prevailing in various parts of the organization. This gives a direct measure of the state of satisfaction of the CHILD in the staff.

► *LEVELS OF CHILD FEELINGS.* Long-range planning is a crucial part of the development and growth as well as change in an organization. Change in an organization is necessary on a continuous basis in order to keep the organization flexible and able to keep pace with a changing environment. If change is not made with careful attention being paid to the human behavioral factors, then fear, anger, and negative stroking will lead to the development of resistance of one sort or another. Hence, an important set of variables to monitor are the fear levels, trust levels, and negative stroking levels in the organization. Some of the best ways to sample these variables which can be elusive to measure in a repressive organizational structure, are through the informal organizational structures, in other words, those old and established employees who are known and trusted by their fellow workers, and via the grapevine, the informal lightning-fast communication system that grows inside every organization as an alternate path for information flow.

These last measurements are more accurate specifiers of what is going on, than the commonly used term "morale" which is difficult to define and has a mystic quality about it.

CRISIS VARIABLES

Another problem that comes up frequently and can affect organizational efficiency is that of crisis. Crisis occurs regularly in any active organization that is interacting vigorously with its environment. A source of funds is suddenly affected, a large order or a new program is suddenly encountered, a strike threatens or occurs, a major storm, earthquake, or other natural disaster occurs, or an epidemic occurs. Any number of things can cause crisis in an organization. The question is "How do the management and staff respond to the crisis?" Collecting data on successful or unsuccessful resolution of crises is an excellent measure of the ADULT functioning of the management and staff. In crisis, individuals and organizations tend to fall back under pressure of fear and hurt, to the CHILD confusion and fantasy if there has been a history of PARENT-CHILD conflict, repression, and oppression. Hidden fears and distorted reactions tend to surface

193

and interfere with ADULT operation. Crisis can also be hidden as if it were some unnatural and unmentionable effect instead of the natural result of living.

Some crisis variables to be measured are the openness with which crisis is greeted, ADULT operation, presence or lack of panic, and presence or lack of PARENT moralizing.

TOLERANCE FOR DIFFERENCE

In any family, group, or organization there exist differences among the members, differences in taste, differences in experience, differences in tradition and moral values, differences in what is fun and creative, differences in temperament and emotional response, and many differences in reactions to the same situation. An important variable which affects the operation of a group of people is the methods that they use to react to the appearance of differences.

For some, differences break the monotony, bring in variety in ideas, spread around different choices of work, and in general are a positive attribute. For others, differences represent a threat of competition, a source of angry reaction, a desire to eliminate the source of difference, a desire to run away from difference—and are seen as a negative attribute. As differences will occur nevertheless, an important measure of the ADULT operation of an organization lies in how it utilizes or avoids differences.

Some of the questions to be answered by management and staff about the organization are:

1. Are differences considered a positive or negative attribute?
2. How does the management react to new or different ideas and approaches?
3. Are staff members hired with an eye to difference or to sameness?
4. How do the organizational PARENT, ADULT, CHILD react, think, and feel about differences in individuals, procedures, structure, and so on?
5. Does the CHILD of the staff feel that difference

194

is liked or disliked, tolerated or not tolerated in the organization?

Measurement of these and other similar effects will tell how open to change the organization is, what its defenses against change are likely to be, and also from what parts of the organization resistance is to be expected. This, of course, can prove to be crucial knowledge in a program of organizational change.

MONITORING OF CHANGE, RENEWAL, AND GROWTH

Finally, how are change, renewal, and growth to be monitored and measured by an organization?

► *GROWTH.* In a profit-making organization growth of the business can be tied to financial growth of earnings, cash flow, sales, or any number of other recognized measures of growth. Growth of productivity, growth of efficiency, and growth of staff size are other measures. Growth in motivation, growth in enthusiasm, growth in interest and involvement are behind these above-mentioned growths and may be measured by interview and questionnaire to the management and staff, provided that a sufficient atmosphere of trust with assurance of confidentiality of response exists so that accurate information is given.

► *CHANGE.* Change is best measured in relation to a long-range planning program. Objectives and goals are set, and change is a result of efforts to reach the preset goals and objectives. The kind of changes which are needed are also a product of long-range planning. Staff and management can determine from time to time what changes have occurred in their functions and in the way that they go about their jobs. Interpersonal changes are determined from change in the type of relationships that occur, and in the changing percentages of various types of transactions, P-P, P-C, C-P, A-A, C-C, and so on. A simple set of questions along these lines will determine change in types of transactions occurring.

A further type of change useful to measure is how staff and management see and rate themselves. Has their self-esteem (i.e., self-stroking) increased or decreased?

What about self-nurturing or patting on the back? Do people in this organization give themselves credit for what they do or do they cnly find fault with their lack of perfection? Change in the permission to use their Nurturing PARENT can be determined by interview or questionnaire.

In the third part of Chapter Ten a list of required changes was given. Each of these changes can be monitored.

► *RENEWAL.* Renewal is a continuing problem for the manager. Life moves on, and what was completed yesterday gives way to what the goals are for today and tomorrow. The cycle of life never stops. When motivation, interest, or growth stop and rigidity sets in, then personnel, staff, or management must be renewed or replaced in the long run. This is the problem of the aging staff and it usually has little to do with the aging process. As the CHILD remains in each human being for his entire life, the potential for excitement, reinforcement, and the encouragement of growth by positive stroking remain a potential that can always be tapped as long as physical disability does not interfere.

Those of the staff and management who are in need of renewal are usually known to the management as well as to themselves. When new excitement and motivation arise in an experienced man or woman, the results are obvious. The lack of a program of re-education, re-motivation, and rewarding among long-term members of an organization is a very costly omission as these experienced personnel are not easily replaced or very quickly replaced, if only for humanitarian reasons.

196

The one who best knows his level of interest and stroke achievement is the person himself, so this information can be determined by simple questioning along these lines. Again, trust level must be high or else no one will admit to lack of interest or motivation.

CONCLUSION

Effectiveness of management can thus be measured and evaluated by using the simplifying Transactional Analysis theory. Ego state response can be obtained and sorted out. The crucial opinions of the CHILD ego can be determined and the question answered: Is management doing its job; and as a result, is the organization dying or growing and flourishing?

Index

Index

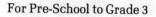

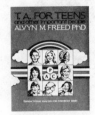